SAILING BARGE MASTER

Published by Chaffcutter Books
in association with the Society for Sailing Barge Research
on Thursday 1st October 2009

ISBN 978-0-9560596-0-4

Images are credited to their source and copyright holder in the Picture Source index. Although the origin, provenance and ultimate source of some images remains obscure, every effort has been made by the publisher to identify copyright holders and obtain appropriate permissions for their inclusion in this publication.

Some photographs are from poor quality originals, but are included here because of their historical relevance.

Society for Sailing Barge Research,
Fleur de Lis Heritage Centre,
10-13 Preston Street, Faversham, Kent, ME13 8NS

Chaffcutter Books,
39 Friars Road, Braughing, Ware, Hertfordshire SG11 2NN

Printed and bound in Great Britain by
Piggott Black Bear Ltd.,
The Paddocks, Cherry Hinton Road, Cambridge CB1 8DH

Around 50 years ago, a group of enthusiasts recognised the importance of recording the fast diminishing number of sailing cargo vessels operating in the coastal and estuarial trades of our island nation. They logged the hulks, laid-up craft and the active fleet of the Thames sailing barge genre, and founded the Society for Spritsail Barge Research. Since that time the Society, now renamed the Society for Sailing Barge Research, to reflect a broadening interest in other cargo carrying sailing vessels around the coastline, has continued to investigate the history of the barges themselves, the way of life of those who crewed in them and the ports they served. In the years since its founding, the Society and its members have so far published around a million words and five thousand photographs on the subject.

Cargo carrying under sail finished in 1970, and whilst a small number of the Sailormen, as the craft and their crews were collectively known, continued under power for a few more years, now just a handful survive in active commission, charter parties and business guests replacing the grain, coal and cement cargoes of yesteryear. Though recognised as an important part of our maritime heritage, today's costs of preservation and restoration appear beyond the scope of many owners; craft that were active in the recent past, now destined to be hulked or broken up, the modest current fleet continuing to dwindle towards potential extinction.

The Society's fortunes, however, seem headed in the opposite direction, with membership continuing to grow. For just £15 per annum, retired and present day bargemen, amateur sailors, academics, students, artists, model-makers, those with family connections, enthusiasts of every hue, enjoy getting the twice-yearly magazine Mainsheet and Topsail, the annual historical publication of the Society. Members are also able to make use of the Society's ever-growing Archive, where more than 10,000 photographs and documents are preserved for the interest of the membership and future generations.

Join us and enjoy the heritage of the sailing barge. An application form appears at the end of this book.

Dedicated by his family to George Winn,
for taking the trouble to leave us this rich legacy.

SAILING BARGE MASTER
Capt. George Winn

The Story of a Victorian Bargeman

Edited by Richard Walsh

CHAFFCUTTER

ACKNOWLEDGEMENTS

This is a remarkable story for a number of reasons. Firstly, it is from a manuscript written between 1934 and 1949, finished just two years short of the author's death aged 82, which has somehow survived to the present day. Secondly, these 146 hand-written foolscap pages were penned by a sailing bargeman who went to sea aged eight, after just two years of formal education, a significant proportion of which was missed through truancy. Thirdly, it covers in depth, and at first hand, a period in the river and coastal sailing barge trades which has never previously been recorded in such a detailed and personal way.

It came to light through a family history enquiry from Joanne Drake, Capt. George Winn's great-grand-daughter, to John White, the Secretary of the Society for Sailing Barge Research. The Society receives three or four such enquiries every week but, unlike most others, this one brought with it a myriad of photographs and documents and, from George Winn's grandson, David Juniper, a family heirloom, the manuscript which forms the basis of this book. Barging was in the family; fathers and sons, brothers and cousins, many following a career afloat as crew member, skipper, or even as owner of sailing barges.

I would like to express my gratitude to all in the Winn family, and particularly Jo and David, for their commitment and enthusiasm in helping to bring this important contribution to our maritime history into print. Thanks should also go to all those who have provided illustrations and other help, in particular to Hugh Perks for the use of photographs from his book, 'George Bargebrick Esquire', about George Winn's long term employer, Messrs. Smeed Dean & Co. of Sittingbourne. Thanks also to Ken Garrett for unravelling a mystery over abbreviations found in some 100 year old correspondence and thanks also to Barry Pearce for proof reading, good advice and corrections. Others, too many to name individually, will know who they are and I trust will accept this expression of appreciation.

Some of the spelling and grammar in the original manuscript has been corrected to aid the reader, though much of the narrative remains unaltered in order to capture the social context of George Winn's writing.

Richard Walsh
Braughing
2009

CONTENTS

Vessel's names are printed in *italics* throughout. Brief details of vessels mentioned are included in footnotes and, where known, further expanded in APPENDIX A.

INTRODUCTION

Grand to be alive isn't it, with memories in the forefront of a grand life, with the halfpenny card nights by the hundred, with perhaps a smack in the gob thrown in, happy and not a care in the world.

If the fathers of our last two beloved Kings and their beloved Queen wives had only been Thames bargemen, what a high load of care and worry they would have been spared. Someone has to do their job, I suppose, and how often I have thought how pleased I am that it wasn't me - and happy to record it. My spritty barge life was a grand experience and not easily forgotten.

If one is fortunate enough, as I am, to live until eighty years of age, after roughly 57 years of this lark, without including the overtime, then one hasn't done bad.

I'm still with my Rosie, my sweetheart bride, she's sitting here with me now; just one night at the Music Hall, that's all it seems, now 62 years since we first met. If she hasn't done any pumping, she's done a bit of washing since then. Now there's just time to get 'two and one' at the Fish Shop, proper daft to get old isn't it? But everyone has to pay that penalty, those of course who live long enough.

And this is largely what I'm driving at; some people live all their lives and see nothing, but are happy as a lark. How do you account for that - is life what you make it, or does fate make it for you? You'll know what I think if you read on. Sometime you will remember the man that was superstitious and wouldn't pass underneath a ladder, and while he was passing by it the other side the painter dropped a pot full of paint on him. Daft, isn't it, but you cant help laughing, can you?

Much of my spritty barge life was with Smeed Dean & Co. By now the directors, the manager, Bob the Foreman, all in the graveyard. It makes you think, doesn't it, of a concern that was once a theatre of joy and laughter, and myself one of the actors of that theatre writing this, and me feeling the strain of wear and tear of a strenuous life, but a happy one. But when you're in trouble boys, laugh it off - there's no other way out of it. Life's a lottery and fate is the master. My experience in life has taught me nothing else, so smoke your pipe and follow me closely, I'm eighty years of age and these days I could eat much more than I can get. It takes me back to my boy days of 1878 when mother and father couldn't afford to give me and Bill, my brother, more than a few potatoes and half a bloater between us. When I started out all those years ago you could almost stand up on the gravy they call our River Thames, now you can see bottom in ten fathoms of it.

One pound going in one pocket and two pounds going out of the other pocket, almost indefinitely, was never going to make me rich. My name is George Winn, the red sail Thames spritty bargeman and old age pensioner, the millionaire without money. It's for you to answer the question whether it's a fault of mine, or the fault of the hand that put the tail on the cow. If those who lose can laugh, what better off are those who laugh that win. I have some idea as to what you might say, but don't you believe it; this is my story and I'm sticking to it, blow high or blow low.

Captain George Winn
Westcliff-on-Sea
1949

White Hart Court, south-side of Duke Street, had back-yards facing the riverside, this photograph taken from Battersea Bridge c.1870. The Adam & Eve Tavern was in the middle of the 'Court' with river access for watermen. Danvers Buildings are thought to be the premises behind the tree to the right of centre. The Ordnance Survey map of 1869 shows the Adam & Eve (*P.H.*) on the river and the White Hart to the north of the ferry hard, next to Old Ferry Wharf, also known as Allen's Lime Wharf, where bricks, drain pipes, chimney pots and lime for mortar were unloaded from sailing barges.

© Crown Copyright MC100037493

CHAPTER I   DEAR OLD WHITE HART COURT

My name is George Winn, I'm a Master Mariner and this is my life story, as recalled from my memory and experience. My mother's name was Maria Winn and my father's name was William Winn. I had two sisters and one brother, the eldest of my sisters was Fanny and the second Eliza, my brother was William, and I'm the baby. I have heard people say that my parents didn't make a bad job of it, so I must give them credit for something! I was born on 22nd February 1869 at our home at 3 Danvers Buildings, White Hart Court[1], Duke Street, Chelsea, London.

I will begin my story in 1873, while I am in petticoats and on Old Tom Tidler's Ground[2] playing Cherry Ogg[3] with a pal, one of the Titherlys. There was Harry Titherly and Arthur Titherly, but which one of them two I can't be sure, but if my memory serves me rightly it was Harry, and he too was in petticoats. Well, what do I mean by Old Tom Tidler's Ground? Our favourite spot was under old Weston's window next to the White Hart Court, Chelsea, and the White Hart Public House was the other side of the Court, down river side. I don't know the name of the people that kept the White Hart. Tom Tidler's Ground reached from Beaufort Street to Church Street so far as me and Titherly was concerned, but the Cherry Ogg gambling spot was always under old Weston's window. We were a bit of a nuisance sometimes, no doubt, but old Weston couldn't say much because he kept a sweets-stuff shop and if he had too much to say he wouldn't have got our farthings. Anyway, I've got no complaints to make about old Weston, and as far as I know I don't think Titherly has either. I can well see the old toff, with his white apron, at least it was made of white material, and his whiskers all around his face and which passed under his chin, and his old pipe. He would stand at his door, for no other purpose than watching us kids, especially if it was Saturday.

---

[1] White Hart Court was a row of residential properties with the Adam & Eve Tavern in its midst, all backing directly onto the River Thames, bounded to the west by Battersea Bridge and to the east by Old Ferry Wharf, which was opposite the White Hart public house. It is recorded that '..the inhabitants obtained drinking water from buckets dipped into the often-polluted River Thames.' Not surprising therefore that five cholera cases occurred in White Hart Court just twenty years before George Winn was born there. Thomas Carlyle's description of Chelsea in 1834 reads 'A singular heterogeneous kind of spot, very dirty and confused in some places, quite beautiful in others…'

[2] Tom Tidler's Ground: Originally a children's game, a phrase which has come to mean land or tenements in a poor district.

[3] Cherry Ogg: An old children's gambling game where cherry stones are aimed at a small target or hole; also as Cherry Hogg, Cockney rhyming slang for Dog.

There wasn't many families in White Hart Court; it was like a little colony on our own. What a home. If ever there was, or is, a heaven, it was the White Hart Court, Chelsea. I can well see and hear the echoes of Old Mother Lewis, one of our natives, at everybody's beck and call. Her Christian name was Margaret. I can't remember her ever having a handkerchief but, to my pride and joy I can see her in my memory in her apron, which she used for many things, with her snuff box, which in those days was well in vogue. Margaret Lewis did washing and was by no means the village idiot; let anyone touch us kids and Margaret was up for No.1 if she was about, as well as always knowing where to raise a couple o' bob on Monday morning. Neither would she shake her head at a little drop of gin. I think that was the usual stimulant of our Court. At any rate that was Margaret's favourite when people made more underclothes dirtier than usual, otherwise

Seen from the top of St. Luke's Church, Chelsea, looking west c.1870, White Hart Court, Duke Street ran from the right of Johnson's Coal Office (centre of picture) to Beaufort Street which formed the approach to Battersea Bridge. Whilst Duke Street was home to housing and businesses, it was very run down, with great dereliction. Seen in the background are Cremorne Gardens, with opulent merchant houses at the opposite end of the social scale.

she wasn't particular once or twice a day with the jug, and no, she hadn't got a moustache - she was alright in that way!

Now as I have already said, there wasn't many families, I think only four in the White Hart Court. There was the Heaths, the Winns, old pal Piper and Margaret Lewis, and I don't think any of them was exactly teetotallers, but Margaret was more noticeable than the others. And Maria, who I haven't mentioned, was my dear mother, Margaret's favourite pal.

Now we'll come to some of the business people on Old Tom Tidler's Ground, that is the ground from Beaufort Street down to Church Street. I don't know who kept the corner public house at the bottom of Beaufort Street, which was named The Beaufort, but starting to work down towards Church Street, Mrs. Hay kept the stationers and tobacconist and that was the first one. Mrs. Farr that kept the greengrocer's shop was the second one and then there was the cook shop, third. Next was Mr. Weidner, the butcher, and Georgie Weidner used to serve in the shop with his father; then there was old Weston's the sweets-stuff shop, the fifth along.

Then it was the pub called the White Hart sixth, next to that Morrison's the oil shop. Now we are about down to Danvers Street[4], and on the other side of Danvers Street, on the corner, there was

Spells, the baker, and next, there was Stevens the grocer, and then Mrs. Maunder's fish shop, and The Rising Sun, a public house. Then came Bulmer, the barber, the dirty dog, I've not forgot him, then an antique shop, and then we are about down to Church Street.

Mr. Weidner was the family butcher and was noted for his pease pudding and fagots and his black puddings. Mr. Spells, the baker, was noted for his seedy cake what he used to give us to make weight, and oftimes would give us a bit to eat out of kindness when we went for a 2lb. loaf, and this was the attitude of all the business people from Beaufort Street down to Church Street, near Cheyne Walk, Chelsea.

Farnfield, the cheese-monger's corner shop, is to the left of the photograph, and marks the start of White Hart Court which extends along the narrow Duke Street to Beaufort Street. This is all George's 'Tom Tidler's Ground'.

[4] Danvers House, demolished in 1696 to make room for Danvers Street, was the Chelsea residence of Sir John Danvers M.P., born 1585, died 1655, and named after him, as was Danvers Buildings, birthplace of George Winn. Sir John Danvers signed the death-warrant of Charles I in January 1649, last British monarch to be executed.

Looking to the east from White Hart Court into Lombard Street, past Spells, the baker, Johnsons, the grocers, Mrs. Maunder's fish shop and Bulmer, the barber, towards Arch House which spanned the road at the west end of Cheyne Walk, with St. Luke's Parish Church in the distance.

And now I am sprouting along, my petticoats are getting short on me and my hair long, white, and curly. The time has arrived for my parents to consider removing my petticoats, to replace them with Knickerbockers, in 1873 for I am now 4 years old. I can well see my dear mother and Margaret Lewis, who's apron strings I hung on to (God bless her), admiring my new attire what they had just fitted on the kid they gloated over, and who either one of them would have laid down their life for. There was two of these knickerbocker suits, one was made of velvet with pearl buttons, and the second suit made of blue material with brass buttons, and both suits bought at the same time. I should say I had but little sleep that night. With all the joys of that day, the sorrows to come were little thought of. Within a short time of my new rig, I had to go with my sister Fanny to Bulmer, the barber, to have the white locks cut off. Of the two happenings, I would have sooner been without the new suits, but it had to come. I can still hear Mr. Bulmer and his men friends passing remarks to each other on my long white locks, which he was about to receive.

But I got over it, as one does everything else in life, and the time rolled on and the next consideration was school. I commenced my education at Park Chapel School at the top of Danvers Street (or at the top of Beaufort Street) and so did my pal Harry Titherly, and later on I will tell you more about my days during my short stay at Park Chapel School, Chelsea.

Chelsea was my native place and home, where the sound of some of the typical people's voices rattle in my ears to this day - those people who used to go about Chelsea selling their wares. There was a man who had something in the shape of a fishing boat the upper side of Lindsay Jetty and he used to sell red herrings, five for a threepenny bit - quite noted for his enterprise. He was one of the people, among others that I am about to mention, who one couldn't forget after buying some of his herrings, because soon after one had eaten them, the most needed thing for the next twenty-four hours was water, or whatever one drank. His cry of "Fine Yarmouth, Fine Yarmouth 'erring" is music in my ears, even today.

Duke Street from Beaufort Street with White Hart Court on the right, Two large lanterns identify the Adam & Eve pub. The white buildings in the distance are the premises of Allen's Lime Wharf. All this was demolished by the late 1800s.

One of the other noted characters was the man who went about at particular times of the day selling pies. His voice would ring as he shouted "Pie, hot." and his cry would echo in the buildings. If by chance he wasn't heard, the hue and cry went around as if someone was drowned. "Where's the 'Pie, hot.' today?", but he would turn up, even if it was nearing midnight. "Where you been all day, boat race[5], eh?" "Pie, hot. Want two?" "No, one." "All right cocky, don't be cheeky. One penny, there you are." "Pie, hot." and off.

The nineteen arch Battersea Bridge was built of wood in 1771. It became the first lighted at night by oil lamps, replaced by gas in 1824. Its narrow arches caused great problems for vessels, even after a central pier was removed and two spans combined in 1873. Ten years later it was closed to traffic, deemed unsafe, and was replaced by the present bridge in 1886.

And there was the woman with the disfigured face, and on crutches, who had lost her husband, that went about selling watercress; all these went to make Chelsea what it was. With her pitiful cry "Jack, he's dead." she would yell. Us kids, knowing the ropes as we did, would stand clear and annoy and tease her, squeaking out to her "Why don't you bury him, then?" and she would up crutch at us, without any good results, of course, and off we go looking for the next one round our street.

So me and Titherly have been going to Park Chapel School for some time now, and for some reason or another we took an afternoon off and didn't reach as far as Park Chapel School, but went down Greaves' boat raft instead. The raft was just above Battersea Bridge, about two minutes walk from our Court, and I can well remember we didn't put in all our time there, because Mr. Walter Greaves wouldn't allow us to be on the

---

[5] Boat Race: Cockney rhyming slang for Face, here probably used as an insult.

raft if he sees us. Not because he was angry, but because he was afraid we should fall in the Thames. So me and Titherly decided to be making our way back towards White Hart Court. We either asked someone the time and they deceived us, or we misjudged the time we had been on parade, so instead of it being something after four o'clock when we would have been expected home, it was some bit before. As we are nearing our Court, my dear sister Fanny, the filthy cat, grabbed me and escorted me home to my mother. I don't know what become of Titherly. So imprisonment

commenced straight away for me. My mother was ill, and me locked in a lumber room, so I'm in some fix, but fortune favours the brave, and the visiting lady came to see mother and she learnt the worst about me, and pleaded for me, and I got released, but not acquitted.

Looking east along Linden Road from Greave's boat raft just west of old Battersea Bridge, where skiffs were built both for sale and hire, and where George and his chum, Titherly, played truant from school.

So next morning the summons arrived from Park Chapel School to show cause why I wasn't at school the afternoon before. The boy that brought the summons from the school seemed well pleased with the honour to bring it. But it wasn't the end of it, so to school I went to face the penalty if there was any. There certainly was, but I didn't know it until twelve o'clock when all the other kids went home and I didn't. One day, without any option, dry bread and water and some red wooden bricks to play with until four o'clock.

So help me God, I certainly forgave my dear sister Fanny, the big cat, but never forgot her, nor dear Old Mother Lewis pleading with teacher for me, but no luck for a reprieve. Yes, I dearly loved her, Old

Park Chapel was built in 1724, its Sunday School commencing in 1814. This became the first National School in the district, known as Park Chapel School for boys. A Park Chapel school for girls was also set up, the combined roll numbering 150-200 pupils. This sketch is by Alfred Beaver, drawn in 1891 and included in Memorials of Old Chelsea by Beaver, published in 1892 by Elliot Stock.

Mother Lewis as a kid, and she loved me, and I have never lost that love for her. The sooner the people straighten themselves out with humanity, the sooner we shall realise the meaning of true love and its worth. If ever there was a God given creature on God's earth it was Margaret Lewis, White Hart Court's Godmother.

And now the time is near at hand to say goodbye to Park Chapel School and the dear old White Hart Court, Chelsea. I'm about 6 years of age now. My father, William Winn, was a bargeman and he was Captain of one of Mr. George Smeed's barges called the *Edward*[6]. There was quite a number of these barges that sailed out of Milton Creek, Sittingbourne, Kent, belonging to various people, and later on I shall tell you more about them.

Now the barge *Edward* had arrived at Lindsey Jetty, Chelsea, and discharged a cargo of bricks. With the permission of the owner, Mr. George Smeed, our furniture was put on board and taken down to our new home at Sittingbourne, including my mother and brother and my two sisters. Although with tears in our eyes, the old White Hart Court, Chelsea, and Margaret Lewis, was never forgotten. My father used to ply between Sittingbourne and Kingston with bricks, or flints and refuse, or manure back to Sittingbourne to complete the voyage, so we often had a run to the old White Hart Court when times permitted.

---

[6] *Edward* of Faversham, built Sittingbourne 1841, 36 tons, broken up 1880. - See APPENDIX A.

Lindsey Jetty at Chelsea showing a topsail barge being unloaded around 1865. A stumpy barge lies across the end of the jetty, probably waiting her turn, whilst two more barges, gear lowered, occupy the river. Battersea Church is seen on the south bank. Note what appear to be barge match winner's pennants flying at the sprit end of both craft. With the Thames Match inaugurated in 1863, their inclusion is probably artist's license, but maybe these barges, painted by Walter Greaves, had been successful in a recent match.

CHAPTER II   HAPPY BOY DAYS

Remarkable to say, our new home was one of Muggleton's Cottages situated dangerously close to a White Hart public house, kept at that time by a Mr. or Mrs. Rook, or both; but unfortunately there was no White Hart Court, and no old Weston's sweets-stuff shop - but the name White Hart eased matters a bit. Arrangements was made for me and my brother William, and my two sisters, to go to the National School situated on The Butts, near the High Street, Sittingbourne. Brother Bill was two and a half years older than me, and our stay at school was quite a short one. It seemed no place for us because my father wanted us with him to man the ship and I never stepped foot in a school after I was eight years of age, and so became one of the crew of the good ship *Edward*. Me and Bill answered as Mate and I think father took on rather a bigger job than he imagined, but money wasn't too plentiful so something had to be sacrificed, and that something was our education.

But before I go on with my sailing barge life I'd like to mention one or two instances about the dear old Upper Thames and one or two people who was second to none at their job; at any rate they had tall ideas that they were. There was a large number of passenger steamboats plied between London Bridge and Kew, perhaps between thirty and forty of them with various names, of course. They were called *Citizen A* or *Citizen B* and so on up to *Citizen N* and, I might say, I had two half-brothers acting as deputy Captains to that Company, and I think Tom Golder, another of my half-brothers, was permanent Captain at that time. All spick and

A Citizen steamer stops for passengers at the Battersea Bridge Pier around 1875. They were known as the 'penny steamers', that being the fare from London Bridge to either Lambeth or Vauxhall piers. By this date passenger levels were already in serious decline on account of the fierce competition from the new tram and rail services. By the mid-1880s nearly all the passenger steamer services on the Thames had ceased.

span men, from the Captain down to the Call Boy, and Captain Cuff was 'It' amongst the other Captains.

I don't know whether his name was Cuff or not, but that was the name he was known by - perhaps because he was noted for his collars and white cuffs, and you never saw him on board without them. Now I've mentioned the word Call Boy; in those days these steamboats never had any telegraph leading to the engine room, so the Call Boy answered for that purpose. These boys was either the son of the Captain, or of the engineer, or the mate, as preference. This boy would stand behind, or rather, abaft the steamboat's bridge, and watch the Captain's movements of his fingers and then he would shout down to the engineer in the engine room what was signalled by the Captain. Just the movements of the Captain's fingers in a certain way, of course only known to them, and never a word spoken by the Captain to the boy. These actions was carried

Aboard the steamboat, with the raised steering position ahead of the funnel, Captain and Mate by the wheel, lifebelts placed on the paddle boxes and on deck, but easily out-numbered by the passengers.

out when approaching a Pier or at any place where they was going to remain stationary up or down the Thames. Imagine we are approaching one of the piers and the boy with his eagle eye is watching the Captain, all typical Londoners. All of a sudden the boy would shout down to the engine room "Ease 'er...stop 'er, go on 'ead." and the steamer was alongside the pier, taking on her passengers and putting off others. Ready to leave the pier again, the boy would shout down the engine room when starting "Go on 'ead."

Then he would go on about his business because he had plenty of other jobs to do until they was about to arrive at another pier. At the end of the day all these steamers would finish up at their moorings opposite the company's yard just above Battersea Bridge, Battersea side, between the hours of 8 and 11 o'clock in the evening, until the next morning. Starting off again early the next day, they run all the year round and on Sundays.

When some of these passenger steamboat Captains had Sunday off duty, they wanted a decent place to get about and be seen in. Baron Rothschild wasn't to compare with them Captains, especially Captain Cuff, more so if the Company was about to have a new steamer and he knew he was going to be Captain of it. A gold signet ring on the small finger of course, with a cigar when going to the Oddfellows or Foresters Club, bursting to sing 'She is the Belle of the Ball, me Boys' which was an old favourite song in those days. And not to forget the Chairman with his ivory mallet to sound the 'Encore', and three cheers for Captain Cuff and his Wife. Captain Cuff could have floated through the air.

And also not to forget the typical Brentford men, smart in themselves and smart with their barges. They were those men in the small sailing barges, about 70 tons, that went farthest down the Thames, going to sea as they would call it, but there weren't only one, or two, there were lots of the sea-going Brentford barges and they were stumpies, that is to say they had no topsail. When they did go to sea that was often as far as Thames Haven, or rather opposite there, known as the West Blyth. They would load some sand there and they would throw it in their barges themselves until she was loaded, and then back they would go to Brentford, and if they happen to arrive home on Saturday, or any other day for that matter, there would be plenty of room on the pavement in Brentford High Street for other people got off in respect of them, and they were all good boys as well, and knew their job.

But when Jack's ashore, what ho, it's the calling that causes the temperature to rise some degrees higher than the average man, because we all think, or rather, most of us think we can do our job better afloat than the other chap. When one barge hits one of the Thames bridges and the other fellow's doesn't, then one would not only have to get off the pavement, but off the Earth also for the time being, to let the other chap past that missed! I'm only including sailing barge men and lighter men, a pretty good combination and I should think it hardly necessary for their boys to go to school in those days, because when a sailing barge fouled a lighter in the Thames he couldn't be off learning something. You would be surprised what some of them know without ever going to school; it seems more of a gift than anything else.

So, in 1878 me and my brother William, known as Bill, as I have already mentioned, joined the sailing barge *Edward* with our father, and mother was pretty often with us too, more because of our youth and mother love. So, we have begun to earn our living plodding to and fro from Sittingbourne to various places in London and taking our chances with the different kinds of weather. Night as well as day was all in the programme, and there were many times sleep was not possible; but when it could be arranged, me and Bill went to bed in the bunk and mother would stay up with father and answer as Mate.

And it's a most God-given life, with our ups and downs and not too much to wear or waste, and for a year or so we didn't turn our nose up at having some boiled potatoes and bread. A few fish or a bucket of whelks from the fishing boats come acceptable, and contentment in those days meant a lot.

Owners of sailing barges back then made it their business to do what they could for their Captains by shifting them into a little bigger and better barge, especially those with a family manned barge. Many of the barges in those days, say in 1875, was small, from 65 tons and upwards but I think not exceeding 100 tons deadweight capacity and very old fashioned, with handspike

Allen's Lime Wharf, adjacent to White Hart Court, takes a brick cargo from Eastwoods' Faversham registered, 1867 built, *Alexandra*. The barge to the right of the photograph, with her gear lowered, possibly having just come up through the bridges under tow or using a 'bridge sail' or under oars, is the *Alabama*, also of Faversham, built 1863.

windlass and all rope standing rigging, and very clumsy and unsightly, with wooden oak tillers. A large percentage of the tillers were an exception to the other tore-out parts of the gear. They were huge pieces of wood sawn out of an oak tree. Often it would take a whole tree to make a tiller, placed in a steam kiln for a week to be able to get the rainbow curve. Then they were artistically fashioned in to shape, some of them with dog's heads at the steering end in the form of the greyhound breed and made of brass. These tillers were very dangerous weapons too. They would fly to and fro across the barge and, accustomed as one was with them, there were many bargemen and barge boys knocked overboard and drowned by them. But it is all in the day's work, and like the steeplejack who would prefer to be at the top of a high smoke stack, there's no more risk attached to one thing than there is to another. From my lifetime's experience of barge work it's just doubtful as to whether there is such a thing as risk; just fate in the main.

Now I am sure you will pardon me for a moment, my brother Bill was born a bargeman, as I was myself, and I can vouch for Bill being knocked overboard, pulled overboard, falling overboard, seven times, and couldn't swim a stroke, yet he died a natural death at the early age of 57 on the land. And we'll say to be correct, at Sittingbourne as boys, I see Bill fall overboard in the River Swale reaching out to get some seaweed to crack[1], but Bill didn't get it and in he went, the tide running about two knots and Bill floundering about like a water logged cat, and me shouting for father. Father rushed out of the cabin, jumped in the boat and picked him up and brought him back to the barge not much the worse for his ducking. I'm not quite sure that Bill didn't get something else, as well as falling in the water, because when mother wasn't on board father didn't take such a lenient view of things. For some reason or other we didn't seem to get off as light if we fell overboard as we did if we smashed our finger or pinched our toe between the boat and the barge, or some other casualty that would happen to us as time went on.

All my comments are based on the difference between risk and fate, and in our boyhood life there seemed but very little difference between our mishaps. If Bill fell overboard I eventually fell in the mud, and when we were sawing and chopping up firewood, if Bill chopped his finger, the saw would fly out of the wood what I was holding and cut my eye and that's what happened on Barnes draw dock at dear old London. I'm proud to say, on our old barge of course, Bill did most of the skippering so far as we were concerned. Never mind about me, I'm only George, the writer of this, and Bill being about 12 years of age and me between nine and ten years of age, what Bill said, went, irrespective of my eye or my head, but we had other things in mind besides sawing and chopping firewood.

---

[1] ...seaweed to crack: 'Pop' weed - Bladderwrack fronds containing air-bladders which give buoyancy to the plant.

We're waiting for the tide to flow, to float our boat that was our most coveted toy, to go boat sailing with our lugsail. But it wasn't a duck[2] sail by any means, it was more often sugar bags cut open and sown together, with a mop handle for a yard. And we are underway now and our sack sail didn't set so badly, and was well admired, and eventually we arrived back to the barge and would talk matters over about improvements - she didn't lay as close to the wind as we wanted her to do, and one could imagine all that took time.

A typical 'river' barge of the mid-late 19th C., the swimmie *Gordon of London*, owned by Robert Miller at Battersea, is seen here unloading into horse-drawn carts off White Hart Stairs, Lambeth.

---

[2] Duck: Untwilled cotton fabric, lighter and finer than canvas, used for yacht racing sails until the introduction of man-made sailcloth c.1950.

In those days the tugboats, such as William Cory's tugs, and others, made an awful noise with chuff, chuffing coming out of the funnel while they were steaming along with their six lighters loaded with coal. So much so, the chuffing marked pretty good time to dance to on the deck of our barge. That being a little in my line it wasn't a bad tune for that purpose and I could manage three with the right and one with the left, and at different times I collected many coppers from the lightermen as they passed close to us.

As well as the thousands of sailing barges, the coal laden lighters were amongst the most prevalent of craft upon the tideway, dozens of Thamesside wharves distributing the coals to merchants, nearby households and local industry.

Now father is about to leave the old *Edward*, and me and Bill of course went with him in another barge in a different firm. We joined a little barge called the *Harry*[3] about 1879, owned by Messrs. Millichamp at Conyer in Kent, and carried on in her for a year. Necessities wasn't too plentiful but as boys we were happy on board our barge and there was always something to occupy our minds. So far as me and Bill was concerned there wasn't any tomorrow to think about.

The *Harry* would be lying in the mud hole or at some other part of the Thames near the City and father would be about his business, getting orders where to take the goods. Having left the barge at 9 o'clock in the morning, he would return back late in the evening. With our day's enjoyment ended, perhaps father not in too good a mood, we'd sit down to tea. Bill would look at me and vice versa, father would do the carving and even if there weren't anything wrong, me and Bill would think that there was. Father

---

[3] *Harry* of London, built Conyer 1868, 28 tons. - See APPENDIX A.

would cut us off a slice of bread each, perhaps two. If he cut us two slices he thought we shouldn't ask for any extra, if he cut one he knew we would ask for more, and a couple of slices of bread and black treacle wasn't to be sneezed at in those days. Father was pretty quiet so I thought I'd venture the question. The worms in my gut were still biting so I asked for another slice; that angered father and he roared out "Ah, you'll have to draw your bloody horns in. I'm not made of money and likely enough we'll have to be underway all night."

And what did that matter; fresh air, something to do, and above all, ambition, that's the stuff that makes men fit for their task. And so we sailed along, year in and year out, me and Bill, him Mate of the barge and George, the writer of these words, is Third Hand, and a time when we didn't know the meaning of the word tired.

So we got plenty of the right stuff that goes to make children into men and, I'm sure you will pardon me for the phrase, little did we think that our time was to be so short with father. Our ups and downs were always about to come to an end. No more scraps between me and Bill on the fore-hatch, out of father's gaze under the leeward part of the mainsail - some times he caught us, and look out when he did. Bill would fly one way and me the other, but father was very lucky if he caught us both at once. But we knew we had got it to come; time didn't count and there was few things in the world more surer than having to face the music.

And so the wheels went around and all in the long day's work, not much less than twenty-four hours a day, pumping and sailing. Still oftentimes we were sorry to have to give up for a few hours on account of contrary winds when our barge couldn't stem the tide, but our ambition ruled in almost all cases, because it was like drawing one's blood to have to bring up[4]. Me and Bill would jump in the sleeping berth for two or three hours sleep and be dead to the world in a matter of minutes, leaving father to keep watch and smoke at his pipe, with perhaps hardly an hour's sleep. And presently father would shout out, "Come on Bill, come on George, we are swung up." or "We are swung down." depending whether we were bound up Thames or down. Naturally it took me and Bill longer to get out of the bunk than it did to get in but, by the time we did get shaped up, father had got the sidelights burning and the kettle boiling. And then we are at it, ploughing the Thames again until we arrived at Hammersmith Dock or Barking Creek, or some other place in the River.

But don't think we are done because we have arrived there. We might get a night's sleep, but it's doubtful even at this stage. No, and all the while you are in one of these red sail spritty barges you are never done with work. You might get a break, but there's always something in mind to be considered, year in and year out for the

---

[4] To bring up: To 'anchor' in the bargemen's language.

duration of the profession, whether it's fifty weeks or fifty years, and I should very much doubt if there is any man in the world who has the amount of strain on him as the skipper of a spritty barge, whether coasting or otherwise.

But I believe it's fate that always decides what will happen. One morning, about 3 o'clock in the year 1880, me and Bill, still with father, are in a fine barge called the *Francis*[5], about 110 tons deadweight capacity, and owned by Mr. Charles Burley of Sittingbourne.

And this particular morning we got underway, bound home to Sittingbourne. We hadn't any cargo and at the time the wind was easterly. We had been brought up in the Thames at a place called Fidler or St. Clement Reach, waiting for high water so that we could proceed down river with the ebb. With sails set spick and span we are standing in towards the shore on the port tack and it was an exceptionally high tide. This was not counted on by father. He was looking for the shore in the dark, which was marshland, and through some error of judgement he was about to wind onto the starboard tack when the barge stopped on the marsh. This was between Swanscombe Cement Works and Broadness and in those days there wasn't any lighthouse on the Point. This was a sad day for us.

Father worried beyond measure and we lay there for seventeen days, telegrams passing to and fro and a tug summoned, called the *Reserve*. She was a large paddle wheel tug

The large paddle-tugs of the 1880s were highly manoeuvreable and powerful craft. Pictured is William Watkin's *Iona*, built in 1876. She was to become the last ship towing paddle tug on the London River. Note the open bridge.

and there were a lot of similar tugs about in those days. A 10 inch rope was passed aboard the *Francis* and a terrific strain applied, but to no good purpose, not a bit did she move, and at the last effort the rope broke, which ended any hope of success. The agreement was £5 if the tug pulled us off and £2 if he didn't. The spring tides arrived again, and the owners had

[5] *Francis*, later *Fanny Maria* of Rochester, built Sittingbourne 1864, 44 tons. - See APPENDIX A.

decided to launch the *Francis* and Mr. Robert Shrubsall of Milton near Sittingbourne undertook the work and succeeded at the top of those tides.

Our barge had taken no damage during her stay on the marsh and I shall add that two other sailing spritty barges called the *Alma*[6] and the *John Bright*[7], owned by Messrs. Smeed Dean & Co Ltd. of Sittingbourne, rendered valuable assistance with their ropes and windlasses in bringing about a satisfactory result. And so, in a day or two we arrived home at Sittingbourne and eventually father was summoned to the Club, for the barge was in the Protection Society. I don't know who gets much protection but that's what they called it, and of course he had to give an explanation of his error. He received little or no mercy and was suspended for six months. That meant he got the sack, but he didn't realise it until the six months had passed and he was refused

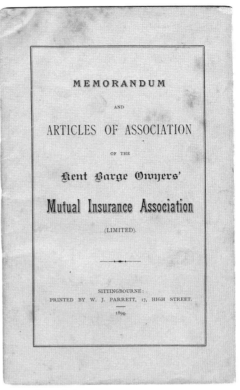

MEMORANDUM

AND

ARTICLES OF ASSOCIATION

OF THE

Kent Barge Owners'

Mutual Insurance Association

(LIMITED).

SITTINGBOURNE:
PRINTED BY W. J. PARRETT, 17, HIGH STREET.

1894.

mastership of the *Francis* ever after. It was a sad and desperate end to our time with our family ship.

Things wasn't too good even at the best of those days, but now we had the worst and it had to be faced and father got a job here and there, but it wasn't an easy task to get skipper once one got out of a berth. The parting of me and Bill wasn't an easy endurance, not only the thoughts of being parted but there was our games to gather and divide, our penny pack of playing cards, our Fox and Geese board[8], and our marbles. The thoughts of mother not being on board with us again, and above all, our boat sailing, what we dearly loved the most, were at an end.

But courage had to dominate and after a short while Bill got a berth as Mate in a little stumpy spritty barge called the *Swiftsure*[9], and a splendid little barge she was, owned by a Mr. Lee of Church Field, Milton, near Sittingbourne. Bill then was about 15 years of age, with his blue Guernsey and pilot cloth trousers and red stockings and headgear, with other boys in the barges

The Protection Society mentioned here was probably the owner's own mutual insurance scheme. Both Charles Burley and Robert Shrubsall were listed among the fourteen directors of the Kent Barge Owners' Mutual, the latter also one of two official surveyors. The Association took upon itself the role of judge and jury over who could skipper the members' barges.

---

[6] *Alma* of Faversham, built Sittingbourne 1858, 36 tons. - See APPENDIX A.

[7] *John Bright* of Rochester, built Sittingbourne 1877, 42 tons. - See APPENDIX A.

[8] Fox & Geese: An old board game for two people, where fifteen white geese attempt to trap the red fox; still available.

[9] *Swiftsure* of Rochester, built Halling 1867, 39 tons. - See APPENDIX A.

they made a fine spectacle; and look out when they was up street on a Saturday night. I'm not sure that some of those boys was Mate with their fathers in small Milton Creek sailing barges, wasn't even a bit younger.

And so the wind blew my brother Bill to London and back time and again with his new adventure, with perhaps 10/- for mother and sixpence for George, but mother was always first, and it began to brighten things up a little. There was a very large fleet of sailing barges that sailed out of Milton Creek belonging to various owners, I should think roughly one hundred and sixty. It was hard strenuous work with unlimited hours, and only a very small percentage of those that tried could carry on, except those that were born bargemen, and who had learned the profession from A to Z.

So months passed and Bill was well away on his own as a full-blown Mate. There were scores of these proud boys, proud of their calling, not only out of Milton Creek but the Medway, Faversham, and Essex. A large number of them had nicknames. I recall Ass and Pockles, and another was called the Duke of Milton, and another was called Whiskers and there was Waistcoat, and there were numerous others I'm sorry I can't remember. And what they had to do was hard beyond belief before a voyage was completed.

And so the time arrived when I joined 'The Fleet', at the age of about 13 years. It was a coincidence that the small barge that I joined called the *Mary*[10], a little 75 tonner, belonged to the same owners as the *Edward*, the barge my father skippered when I was five years of age. The *Mary* was a swimmie and she belonged to Messrs. Smeed Dean & Co. Ltd. of Sittingbourne, Kent. The Captain's name of the good ship *Mary* was Harry Hull and you will understand I am 'Chief Mate' and I could not have gone to sleep that night if someone had given me poison, and so

The Long Reach Tavern was a very isolated hostelry that played host to generations of sailing bargemen. Located on the south of the river just east of the entrance to Dartford Creek, barges which had set out for London from Kent or Essex would carry the tide, anchoring off the Tavern for the ebb, leaving on the new flood to sail to their destination.

down on board I go full of the joys of being Mate. And what a craft - 30,000 bricks and all night out, a lovely moonlit night, sailing along towards King's Ferry Bridge, then to Sheerness and now out to sea, and to plough up the dear old Thames once again. At high water the next day about 3 p.m. we brought up at the top of Long Reach, opposite the Tavern[11] on the south shore, and quite ready for a doze in the dear old

[10] *Mary* of Faversham, built Hammersmith 1819, 29 tons. - See APPENDIX A.
[11] Long Reach Tavern, Dartford Marshes, demolished in the 1960s.

Many small sailing barges delivered and collected cargoes on the capital's Regent's Canal, horse-drawn along the towing path, passing through locks to leave the Thames and often en route to the wharves and basins which served the metropolis. The tow path and bridges were popular meeting places for children who, against all the rules, often swam in the canal, or joined in gambling games.

bunk, that I had missed for so long on account of father's misfortune. It would have taken a number of horses to have got me out for the next six hours to come. And so we are bound to Black Mare's Wharf in the Regents Canal, where we arrived the next morning about 2 a.m. after another 3 or 4 hours sleep. But it wasn't sleep I was thinking about, it was the fifteen shillings that I had got to come for the cargo of bricks, and if we loaded a cargo back, which we did, there was another ten shillings, making it in all twenty-five shillings for just eight days and nights.

What a banquet and what a homecoming for mother with my wages put in her lap. Fresh hope and encouragement for her and a little extra for the table. And father doing a little work on shore straightened things out considerably. For me, to achieve these ends, there was something more to be done than walking the deck with a muffler around one's neck and hands in one's pockets. Towing up the canal from morning 'til night before one arrives at our destination, wet through the greater part of the day, gear to be 'ove up, ready for unloading, and food to be got ready during the day, if you had the luck to have the time to get it. Up and down canal the same thing happened. We were towed up and down by a horse and if the towline got foul, as it often did, the horse driver would swear at me, but we soon got to know that that was his idea of a friendly chat! The Regent's Canal was rather a rough locality and while passing through some of the bridges that spanned the canal, one had to watch out or you would get half a brick or a stone on your head, but that was all in the day's work.

And so we are back home at Sittingbourne after my first voyage as Mate with all the joys and glee of a boy who has just

More than abuse was sometimes delivered from the bridges over the Regent's Canal. Here, a dumb coal barge is towed under a bridge whilst young and old look down from above. Coal was one of the mainstays of the barge trades in Victorian London.

started out on his own, but soon to learn that one was hardly ever done with work, night or day. But me and my brother Bill never had time to consider that, our hot blooded enthusiasm for the red sailed spritty barge work increased in temperature from the fires that had raged in us in previous years.

Me and Bill by chance at times would pass each other in the Thames perhaps, or somewhere between London and Sittingbourne. When we did it was similar to that on an Oxford and Cambridge Boat Race Day, waving and shouting to each other as long as we could, with likely a small bubble in the corner of our eye, and as long as it lasted, I can say for a minute or two, we didn't know there was any one else in the world, all because of the excitement of our previous years with father.

But we soon got hardened to our task, and although most of the skippers were hard men with the barge boys, at the same time they didn't do those boys much harm in the long run. There were fifty or more sail of barges in Smeed Dean alone, and most of the barge boys in our firm grew up and became skippers of the same firm's craft.

I would like to refer you back for a moment to a previous remark regarding fate and the part it plays in life. I am a fatalist, as I understand it, and I have seen instances of how fate plays its hand. For instance, and as a reminder of what I wrote earlier, my father was Captain of the barge *Edward* and for some reason or other he lost the *Edward*, making way for another young skipper to take charge of her. Father loses his command and the new skipper gloats over his turn of good fortune. It's the same the world over; selfishness and intolerance creates an atmosphere that destroys the beauty of life, of which I shall write more. The young skipper as above referred to, known as Harry Broad, and better known as 'Broady', lost his life around 1878 through the capsizing of the *Edward*; also lost was his wife and brother, who answered as Mate, on the Grain Spit near Sheerness. Such is the turn of fate.

Resuming our boy days in the barges, I've known as many as thirty sailing barges leave Milton Creek at one tide, manoeuvring down the West River Swale. One of the sights in barge life well worthwhile seeing was the juvenile Mates with their red stocking headgear and blue guernsey, buzzing about like flies aboard their barges, mopping, scrubbing and a dozen other things to do, and if the boy couldn't do two or three things at once he was harshly dealt with until he could. Shooting King's Ferry Bridge[12] was no child's play and had to be gauged in navigation to the matter of feet, and a box of the ears taught one that. Some of the fleet would get right out to sea first ebb, others would get as far as Queenborough and some only as far as Cod's Reach by the time it was low water. Usually the skippers would decide to bring their barges alongside in twos and threes and fours, and they would gather down one cabin or the other and chat and smoke or chew tobacco, and laugh about something that had happened during the ebb tide.

But never was a boy allowed in the cabin with them but they would be doing the same thing for'ard, arguing as to whose riding light shone the best, or whose cabin was the cleanest, or whose boat was the smartest. "Yours ought to be the cleanest", one would say, "You've got a new mop." "Yes," another would say, "mine looks as good as his and I've only got an old mop." or "Did it hurt you when yer skipper hit yer?" ...and to finish up with, likely as not, a scrap! And so time passed with more or less the same routine. You'd hardly ever see these barge boys smoking a cigarette, only because perhaps they knew the penalty - a smack in the 'chops'.

There were some of the old Captains who never lost sight of us brothers after being parted from our father. Old Captain Harry Wooley, and Captain 'Harry' Pearce and others, knowing all the

---

[12] King's Ferry Bridge connects the Isle of Sheppey to mainland Kent.

circumstances as they did about the affair of father's suspension, played a great part in warming us up from the nip of the frost whenever they came in contact with us. So much so, Bill and I would approach them in thought and deed almost the same as we did father, and there were not anything too hard, or too late for us to do for them. And one of these old Victorian Captains, Captain Pearce to be correct, had three sons in turn Mate with him followed by his grandson, in a little stumpy barge called the *Emily*[13]. There was Tom, Charlie and Alf and never would he address them other than as Thomas, Charles or Alfred, and my brother, William, never Bill, and if it was myself it would be George, of course, and this principle he held beyond measure. I think all the sons became skippers of barges of the same firm. Unfortunately the *Emily* sank at North Woolwich, London, and Captain Harry Pearce and his little grandson that answered as Mate, were drowned - this was in 1894.

Courtesy was a great motto of most of these old barge skippers. Of course they all had their fads and fancies. Only as far back as 1878 there were several of them wore silk top hats. Skipper Steve Hall of Faversham, when up and dressed, wore a silk top hat and frock coat, but it didn't stop him chewing tobacco, and I don't know of any one chewing more. About the same time there was another old skipper, but I don't know his name, who was Captain of the barge *Citizen*[14] of Queenboro'. Rather eccentric old toff he was; I have known him to be steering his barge up Sea Reach standing at the tiller with his silk top hat and frock coat on, which was a rare sight in those days, but I don't think he ever smoked or chewed tobacco. If he was going ashore for a loaf of bread and a quarter pound of butter you could bet he would be dressed up the same before he ventured out to get it.

While I'm passing a few remarks about these old warriors, if a landsman met a few of these old skipper toffs and didn't know their profession, at a guess they would think they were peddlers selling needles and cotton, or mohair bootlaces or paregoric tablets[15]. And to add to these old Victorian skippers there was another noticeable 'bundle of clothes' walking about who represented himself as a barge master, with frock coat of course, but not the topper high hat in this case, but some sort of felt hat with no shape or make, similar to the shape of an umbrella, inside out, scudding before a gale of wind. He was the awkwardest built man I ever set eyes on; his boots, the upper toe part, I can safely say, could have carried a half a dozen marbles in the valleys of each boot without spilling them for as many miles as he liked to walk. With a large prominent nose he was certainly the limit of appearance of any barge skipper I ever saw. He sailed a barge called

---

[13] *Emily* of Faversham, built Sittingbourne 1856, 33 tons. - See APPENDIX A.
[14] *Citizen* of London, built Lambeth 1846, 59 tons. - See APPENDIX A.
[15] Paregoric: An opium based treatment for stomach upsets.

the *Vincent*[16], 75 tons deadweight, owned by Messrs. Smeed Dean & Co. Ltd. of Sittingbourne. He certainly had his own fads and fancies and never copied others. It was no strange thing to see him with his feet in the cooking pot soaking his corns in the 'ock of bacon liquor, but apart from his innocent whims we must give him his dues and by no means was he as dim as he looked to us youngsters. He was a self-taught cabinet-maker and one of the things he made, out of many, was a harmonium. He wrote his own music and could sit down and play it - but as a navigator in the Thames, he only found out the set of the tide when he hit the bridges. As we all shall, he eventually passed away, but the good names of these old Captains still ring in my ears for their fatherly assistance toward me and my brother Bill, after father's disaster with the *Francis*.

The stumpy, *Vincent*, after the combine was formed, when Blue Circle became the cement branding and was applied to the mainsails of all the stumpies and the topsails of the topsail barges.

Time changes all things, and our ups and downs wasn't finished - they had hardly begun. I had made a start in the race of life but was not old enough to know and understand what was taking place in the background, particularly the anxieties of father worrying over his misfortune, which had rendered him more or less idle. I did not know the meaning of the word worry in the way he experienced it, and unforeseen to me, within two years, the strain overcame father and he entered a mental home and there died, leaving mother to our care.

Anchored, the barge's gear has been lowered, the Captain and Mate await a tow up through the Thames' bridges to their destination to discharge their cargo. The enormous tiller is swung to starboard. In the background is Billingsgate, this part of the Thames then below all the bridges.

This worst had to be faced with a sorry heart, but after the night, and 'chin up' as the saying goes, the dawn still came. So we worked with mother to see it through, and still put our wages in her apron, with more zest than ever, and more responsibility than I understood.

[16] *Vincent* of Rochester, built Murston 1879, 35 tons. - See APPENDIX A.

I was 14 years of age by then, with muscles like coconuts, and all ambition, and never expecting things to go wrong, like the girl who made her first cake and forgot to put the currants in it, but my experience taught me different. And so I ploughed along up and down old Father Thames, first in one barge and then in another, the barges being a little bigger each time, and two or three shillings more in wages which was a great asset to us in those days. And on the whole I began to make big strides and between seventeen and eighteen years of age I rose to Mate of one of our firm's First Class barges called the *George*[17], singularly appropriate perhaps, because I'm George, the writer of this story.

These barges were a fine class of craft and there were several of them, some of them new and others nearly new. The barge *George* was Captained by Jack Saxby when I went in her, and although they done hard work by carrying heavy cargoes, many were more like yachts to look at than they were barges. They were painted, gilded and grained up to artistic taste and their cabins gorgeously arranged, so much so that it wasn't an uncommon thing to comb one's hair in the gloss of the wooden panelling.

There was some Mates in these craft, because in passing, I can assure you the competition was too great, that did not measure up, and there were many more Mates defeated than champions. Mates of these particular craft was soon taught to know when they could look at their Captains, and when they couldn't. Although one was hardly ever done with work in these craft, it was no easy job to get a Mate's berth in one of them, but it was more than easy to get the sack, and there wasn't much difference in respect of sacking between the owners and the Captains.

Messrs. Smeed Dean & Co., were a prosperous, go ahead firm, with a Manager probably second to none. His name was Mr. George Andrews. He rose out of his bed about 4.30 every morning; cold water bath, winter and summer, perhaps an egg and brown bread and butter, with hot milk, then down to the stables to give every foreman orders what to do for the day. Some mornings he had 30 sail of barges to cater for and he did so for many years. He was one who took a marked interest in the wellbeing of the barge boys and I am proud and thankful for his guardianship, when Mate and later as Master, after the death of my dear father.

And so, with my ups and downs, I am nearing the end of my happy boy days, probably the cream years of my life. The unforeseen was to follow and my task was to continue, and shortly to become a man and shoulder the world and its responsibilities, but never losing the memories of my young life with the other barge boys, and the girls we had met, as we drifted apart and set our own course.

---

[17] *George* of Rochester, built Murston 1879, 43 tons. - see APPENDIX A.

CHAPTER III   MARRIAGE AND STRIFE

I am 18 years of age and still Mate of the barge *George* and I have now decided to stay with the barging life and to leave nothing undone that would assist me to become Captain. Having sown the greater part of my wild oats, I took unto myself and courted a fine buxom girl for my sweetheart. She was one of Messrs. Edward Lloyd's Paper Mill girls. The Paper Mill was at Milton, but Rosie Houghton, by 1887 my sweetheart, hailed from Sittingbourne. It wasn't love at first sight, as we had known each other for a year or more and she was already attached. I was determined to out-weather the other chap. And so Rosie, with her bustle, and me George, with my black doe skin suit and patent leather boots, done the deed, and we desperately and defiantly fell in love and enjoyed a short, but happy, courtship for two years or so - happy days. There were quite a good number of girls working at Lloyd's Paper Mill in those days, I think I could say about 700, and a jolly sociable crowd, and for some reason or other they would certainly find the barge boys, or vice versa, and many of them married these girls and excellent wives they made, including for myself.

And believe me, we are beginning to make things smoke, and the time has arrived when we would just mention it to the Captain, and to say if it didn't suit him that I would leave. And that is what happened, so I left the *George* and shifted over as Mate into a similar barge called the *Livingstone*[1], still optimistic about shortly becoming skipper. But our dear Manager wasn't too eager about making Mates Captains if one wasn't married, although quite capable of the sailing. So me and my sweetheart talked matters over with her mother and father concerning our marriage, but not with my dear old mother, good gracious no, as it would have been a toss up whether it would have been a wedding or a funeral! So we decided to marry, and I think Rosie's bustle played a great part in the contract!

So we stuck to our ambitions like glue with our young minds working twice as fast as before. Rosie was 19 years of age, and George, the writer of these words, was 20 years of age. The few months passed and the happy day dawned, the 18th December 1889. When I arrived home in my barge at eleven o'clock, the eventful morning began to unfold. Full of life's joys at this new undertaking, with a little two-room palace furnished and arranged, and my average wage 25 shillings per week, but what a day. What a height to rise to, rushing about like the

---

[1] *Livingstone* of Rochester, built Murston 1880, 44 tons. - See APPENDIX A.

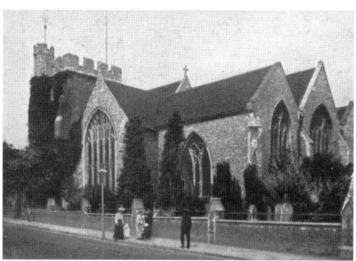

St. Michael's Church, Sittingbourne, where George and Rose were married.

Scottish Express to get home, cleaned up, to take unto myself a wife at 2 p.m. I've been sailing through the night before, and a day's work done in a few hours, but in my joy it was easy and worth it. One didn't get tired in those days; one never had time to get tired. So I arrived at the house in good time and in a short while I am groomed ready for the noble hour, with my bride by my side, also full of the joys of her young life. Flags were flying and the villagers were out, the horse and cab ready, the driver with his whip decorated with white ribbon, and the wedding guests summoned and waiting for the word to go. And so we descended the steps from the house, my bride to be with her father, and me with a lady guest. Of course we couldn't all ride in the cab, so some walked to the Church, St. Michael's, Sittingbourne, to be correct, where we were made Mr. and Mrs. G. Winn.

And what a return journey, Sittingbourne was all aglow, many admirers with their rice throwing, and my dear old mother there, with her hand full of mud! I didn't think she'd throw it, but all the same, she was there with it, sure enough. She was rather a hard nut to crack, but a good old soul on the whole, having weathered a hard life, so we coaxed her eventually, and she joined us at the evening party. I could see in the years that followed, at times she couldn't quite stomach the idea, but her upset faded as time went by.

The happy couple's Marriage Certificate.

Me and Rosie sat on the throne to all comers and so the time arrived to have supper, which took the place of the wedding breakfast and at midnight everyone drank to the bride and bridegroom, and we all sang the last song; it was 'Wait Till The Clouds Roll By, Jennie, Wait Till The Clouds Roll By.'[2]. And we let ourselves go and gave it everything, and then the assembled company retired to their respective homes and me and Rosie to our little home, our palace, our castle.

Mrs. and Mr. Geo. Winn, millionaires without money! As the poet said 'He is a wise man who does not grieve for the things which he has not, but rejoices for the things he has.' Did I shun the old lady with the handful of mud? Oh no, I did not; but she didn't sing the wedding night parting song because she was choked and starved to the bone at the thought of losing her last baby son. I had been attached to her apron strings too long to forget, like my brother and my two sisters. We stuck by her until her last second on this earth, God bless her, and so time masters all things.

The wedding bells have ceased to ring and a few hours sleep is welcomed, then to be up and at it the next morning at 7.30 with a pound of homemade sausages for breakfast, and then away, with a parting kiss, to board my barge, the *Livingstone*. And plans for our honeymoon occupied my thoughts, I tell you, and so on the 19th, after the wedding night before, I sailed again from Sittingbourne to Waterloo, London, with a cargo of bricks, which was the major part of our firm's industry[3]. We arrived on the 21st December, and this was where I decided we are to spend our honeymoon and our Christmas on board the *Livingstone*. And so it was a telegram to Rosie to join me there, to celebrate the greatest event of our lives.

What a picture, as W.W. Jacobs would have it, the Beauty and the Barge[4]. And the world was ours as well, together for the duration of our lives. And in our spare time we would walk out on shore to different parts of dear old London nearby, to do our shopping for Christmas decorations for our cabin. Whether it was at the dear old Canonbury Music Hall or a stroll on the Embankment, every minute was an hour to us. Christmas morning arrived and a pretty busy time ahead of us too, the Christmas pudding to be made and in the saucepan boiling was one of the chief items of the day, not one of mother's Christmas puddings, but a good sound beef steak and onion pudding, and I had made it. What a banquet - the Savoy Hotel never entered our heads. And we had celery for tea; the

[2] Wait Till The Clouds Roll By, words by J.T. Wood; music by H.J. Fulmer, published in 1884, is a song about lovers separated by a career at sea.
[3] Smeed Dean & Company's business was in brick and cement manufacture.
[4] Beauty and the Barge was from the pen of William Wymark Jacobs, a prolific writer of maritime fiction, born Wapping 1863, died Islington 1943.

Houses of Parliament was only a pantry compared to our barge on this Christmas Day. Boxing Day dawned with the same spirit, by now the hours passing like minutes. Breakfast was no sooner cleared away than it was time for the bubble and squeak for dinner, with all our plans laid out for the evening ashore, which me and Rosie are passing at the Tivoli Music-Hall in the Strand.

And we shall never forget that 'do', the crowd and, what a sight, the ladies with their bustles and the boys with their bowlers, and guards and the police keeping order and a right of way, all this was a sight not to be missed. In the crush some of the ladies bustles got round in front, some of them at the side, and Rosie's, God knows what happened to hers, a country girl, but she stuck to me like grim death. When the doors opened, the police went the same way as the people, inside, but we were up in number one for a seat. It was one house a night in those days; Miss. Marie Lloyd, Miss. Kate Carney, Albert Chevalier and Harry Lauder, worth a few 'bustles' wasn't it! Dan Leno, Charles Godfrey and our old George Chirgwin, the White-Eyed Caffer, from eight o'clock until eleven passed like the flash of a gun. And so the bride and bridegroom strolled back to the good ship *Livingstone* arm in arm over Waterloo Bridge repeating and laughing about the wisecracks of the evening.

With the end of our Yuletide festivities near at hand, our decorated cabin is occupied once more, and supper arranged. Although it was odds and ends left from dinner, it didn't go down too badly, with a few tunes on the accordion while Rosie cleared away table and the small hours of the morning all ready upon us. We ended our celebrations and retired to bed for a few hours sleep, not because we were tired, but because we had ended a long happy day, and well broken into another. A few hours sleep in those days, out of each twenty-four, was always a luxury and, if you will allow me, it was in most cases well earned.

And so, 7 a.m., same morning, to be up and at it, more or less with the same routine, with jokes from the workmen, who had known me for a number of years at the wharf, concerning our honeymoon Christmas, and their cheery remarks for us. It was time for breakfast, and then Rosie's time well taken up with a letter to mother and father, and what a lot she had to write, away from home for the first time in her life.

And so half of the honeymoon cruise is over and Captain H. Harvey has arrived back on board from his Christmas holiday, and we are discharging a cargo of bricks, and then we are bound up to Lambeth Vestry Wharf to load a back cargo of refuse for Sittingbourne, which took three or four more days. With the everlasting cooking, scrubbing, sailing and so on, eventually we arrived home at Sittingbourne at Messrs. Smeed Dean & Co.'s Murston wharves.

Soon the bride and bridegroom was indoors with mother and father with more to talk about than I shall be able to tell you here, this being about the last act of the honeymoon cruise. Yours truly and Rosie retired to our little home in Shortlands Road, Sittingbourne to relax for a few hours and to get a breather, and although the cruise had ended, all the fun hadn't by a long chalk. We retired upstairs to bed. We had a nice little bedroom suite, with an iron bedstead decorated with brass knobs and brass roses, which was very fashionable in those days. I don't know whether Rosie had got as far as to don her nightdress or not, but what I do know is that I was sitting on the side of the bed, at the back part of it, taking my socks off when, all of a sudden, down went the bedstead and me

Livingstone, left, and *Young Jack*, deep laden, probably with refuse for brick-making, drift up Milton Creek past Smeed Dean's lower Murston wharves.

with it. It was a brand new bedstead, so help me God. It broke at one of the joints at the end of one of the sides. Fortunately Rosie wasn't in bed; it's common knowledge to know how long it takes a lady to dress and undress. Well, with all the happy hours we'd had on our honeymoon cruise without a mishap, this was the limit. Never, in all my young life, was I so exhausted for breath, at choking point, as one would say, with laughter, and I wasn't alone. Never shall we forget it, had we been in bed before it broke God knows what the shock might have done. So we got a box and put it under and got it fixed up for the time being.

Next morning the landlady see Rosie and asked what was the matter. Rosie showed her the broken bedstead and another neighbour see it. One said one thing and one said another and I wonder now what they was really thinking! There was quite a little gathering around it and the most sensible one of all said I should take it back. Well, we didn't need any advice on that, so Rosie went and see the upholsterer. I didn't go; it didn't want two of us, and he came and saw it and examined it and soon he found what he called a flaw in the welding. In less than no time he sent us another side and no additional charge, and it lasted many years, so many I don't know the end of it now.

In my previous remarks I mentioned the word fate, and fate, as I understand it, is the greatest foundation in my life. I ask you to do me the honour to follow me if you can, to understand what I mean, from the beginning of my writings, here, and on.

'...to and fro, up and down Old Father Thames...' A routine way of life, but different every trip.

So leaving the bedroom disaster behind, I toddle off down onboard again with my food in a long white bag, known among bargemen as the 'Shirt' bag, containing the sea stock; two loaves of bread, half a pound of butter, one pound of cheese, quarter pound of tea, small tin of milk, two pounds of bacon and a cake, if one was lucky, and an ounce of tobacco. Leaving my young wife behind for a week or eight days, it dragged a little, but it had to be faced. I think it took a bit longer for me to get down to the barge than it did to come home, although it didn't do to get far behind or the skipper would soon want to know where you had been; but in my case, for this once, there was forgiveness.

So I carried on as Mate in these barges, with my optimism for a position of command and sailing for myself, as I was looking forward to. In spite of all efforts that flesh and blood could perform, it was not to be. The unforeseen cropped up. Life, it seems to me, is not what one makes of it. It's the good or evil spirit within one that dominates. A person's capability just runs a small part of the machinery of life, he or she unable to dictate the course of it as an individual. The human being is nothing more than a lamp, controlled by an almighty spiritual power. You will burn bright or dim, and you'll go out, but you'll have nothing whatsoever to do with it, at whatever stage of life, or however great your efforts.

And so we paddled to and fro, up and down Old Father Thames, and as you are beginning to understand, our owners were hard masters and very strict, with heaps of work to do for little money, and the men all round suddenly decided that something must be done to bring about a betterment of things - better pay for the work we did. We were already union men[5], and so the heads of the union sent in a list to all the sailing barge owners of what we wanted over and above the current rate of pay, telling them that in the event of the Masters[6] failing to meet us in this respect, we should strike on 1st March 1890.

By now I knew there was between 60 and 70 sailing barges in our firm alone, and hundreds of others in different firms. And so 1st March arrived, and as the barges arrived home and the skippers went into the Office for our money that was due, they were asked whether they were going away again for the current rate of pay. Everybody said 'No' and was told to take their goods and chattels out of the barges and leave them, which we did.

This was a very different tune for me after what had taken place on the 18th December. It certainly looked like the start of a dirty night for us newly-weds. We didn't get butter on both sides of our bread as it was, and our banking account was only thirty-eight shillings. Things didn't look too prosperous for us. If we could manage to float with our mouths above the water it would have to be good

---

[5] The success of the Labour Protection League and the London Dock Strike of 1889 inspired the creation of many small trade unions to protect bargemen. The Bargemen's Protection Society was one such, which took on the brickmasters of Milton Creek.

[6] Masters in this context were the employers, not the captains of the barges. Smeed Dean employed more than 1,000 people in and around Murston.

enough, although our course was altered considerably. There was no choice for the Mates of the barges, as we had to do as we were told, and what the strikers were going to do was appalling, but the promises told to us made some of us boys optimistic, but optimism didn't increase our banking accounts. The second week had passed, and the strikers' meeting had been well attended with a little jollification and a sing-song and so on, full of the joys of spring and hope. So I toddled off home as usual to Rosie, and she gently broke the news that we were bankrupt. Who would have thought it after leading off two weeks previous with a decent balance. Did I scold Rosie? Oh no, we talked matters over and it was just like talking about anything else; we understood the situation and we were as one.

If you'll allow me for a moment, I'd been on the rocks too many times for want of a 'tanner'[7] to think of any thing else but success, as perhaps you have already noted. We were taught by experience, a hard task perhaps, but an excellent school-master, but I wasn't alone in that class. To work two and three weeks with no pay while 'under repairs' to hold onto one's job was normally considered all in the day's work, and if the Mate was behind some mornings then the skipper would let rip at him, and if the poor Mate was married he would tremble like a leaf, frightened he would get the sack. And some actually did get the sack in years gone by for this offence, but they didn't have too much trouble about getting their odd ha'pence[8] in those days. But with a strike and times as they were, something had got to be done about our bankrupt situation, so I marched up to the union chief and stated our case. It was put before the Lodge and carried unanimously that I was to have ten shillings a week strike pay. That brightened things up a little; as my dear old mother used to say, when one door shuts another opens. Fortunately there was only two of us, but it wasn't many weeks after that I found out that mother didn't know everything. As one of our honourable London judges said once, "I may not always be right," he said, "but what I say goes."

So the weeks passed, marching about from one district to another, threatening to floor the world if our masters didn't pay up and look large, with our banners and flags flying. We took to hooting at our Masters, and pelting the blacklegs taking our barges away. Some of the older hands mustered and blocked the Creek. By then, some of the weaker union men went weeping to their masters, pleading to let them take their barges again without an agreement, lowering themselves down to the level of blacklegs. But the Masters refused their assistance. Not only did some of the strikers lack sufficient food, but they needed a clean pair of trousers as well.

On and on it went, with no give on either side. The tenth week of the strike arrived with the whole place teeming with the desperate

---

[7] A 'tanner' was a silver coin worth six old pence, the equivalent of $2\frac{1}{2}$p. today.

[8] A ha'pence was a copper coin the equivalent of 0.2 of the present day One Pence.

Milton Vicarage
Sittingbourne
April 18. 90

My dear Sir
    In reply to your letter of April 17 received this evening I think I had better tell you how things have gone here.
    About the middle of Feb: last the Bargemens union for these waters - Faversham to Rochester - framed a "list of prices" for the brick trade & sent it to the employers with the note that it would come into effect on March 1st
    The Barges trade as per freights per journey - 1/2 going to barge owner 1/2 to Captain & mate.
    The men say that the freights were reduced some years back and that they were promised that the old prices should be restored when the state of the Brick trade permitted. that the time had come and

The first page of a long letter from the resident Chaplain at Milton Vicarage, the Revd. Robert Payne Smith, sent to the Archbishop of Canterbury in reply to his letter voicing concerns regarding the bargemen's strike. In 1890 carbon paper had been in general use for nearly 100 years, but was not very effective when the original was written with pen and ink, nor were carbon copies admissible in court. Church letters were often written twice, once for the addressee, and again in a book as a record, as with this copy. A full transcript appears in Appendix B.

men, and the masters too, at their wits end. Our strike pay had been reduced to just five shillings per week, plus a food ticket, to be exchanged at Mr. Hampton's shop, Milton Regis. This Mr. Hampton was a splendid fellow; he was the bargemen's friend, before and after the strike, especially to young married Mates of the barges. Whether you could pay or not, one was always welcome to his goodwill and we couldn't speak too highly of him. His favours were a big asset to us in harnessing the horse; his shop was half grocers and half outfitters, and again I'll say he was a worthy gent.

But this strife that had befallen our short married lives of only three and half months had to be faced, with the poor helping the poor, with her mother and father on Rosie's side, living from hand to mouth, and me at a dead end. Our leaders kept telling us at the meetings that we were winning, and that there was a rift in the clouds. Some of us didn't want telling that, because we had already realised that we were falling through them wholesale.

During the tenth week of our hardship, to our surprise and joy, the Masters, seeing the difficulties on either side, called a meeting with our union committee. They discussed the trouble with our leaders and settled the dispute by giving half of what they struck for, and recognised the union's rights[9]. But the Masters never forgot what had been done to them. Some of the Captains went back in the same barges, some didn't. My Captain didn't have the same barge again, and they were all scattered about, more or less like lost sheep, to teach them a lesson. It didn't make much difference to me, as I joined a similar barge to the *Livingstone* called *Bessie*[10], skippered by one of the old hands, known as old Bill Saxby. He was a cantankerous old sod, he was, but Rosie always came first, and much had to be swallowed, so there was no real choice. Ambition had to be put on hold.

He was the limit. I would turn out to get breakfast and put the kettle on with the spout pointing to port, and while I was on deck he would turn out and turn the kettle round with the spout pointing to starboard. Although I was known to be able to take my place with the next at the barge game, I don't remember doing anything right for the twelve months I was Mate with this Madame Tussaud's old fossil of a skipper. You heard about the 'Beauty and the Barge' but this was the 'Devil and the Deep Sea' and a year in prison would have been a luxury compared to the twelve months that I served in the sailing barge *Bessie*.

And so, during my hard labour, there was born to us our first baby. But bonnie Georgie[11], my little son, only lived four days in favour of my young wife, and the blow to us was anything but a light one, and not what you need when things wasn't going along too pleasant with me and this old skipper.

These sailing barges were to many the pride of the Thames, and although it was more or less a twenty-four hours a day task, it was somewhat difficult for most of the Mates to keep their berth in these particular craft. They were known as the 'Forty-Twoers', meaning they

---

[9] The story of the 1890 bargemen's strike is told in George Bargebrick Esquire by Richard-Hugh Perks, published by Meresborough Books in 1981.
[10] *Bessie* of Rochester, built Murston 1888, 43 tons. - See APPENDIX A.
[11] George Henry Winn, born 8th March, died 12th March 1891, reportedly as the result of being vaccinated against smallpox.

The sailing barge *Bessie* at work, seen here locking out of the Surrey Docks in her later years. To her left is the *Ada Mary*, like *Bessie*, built at the firm's yard at Murston and both long serving members of the Smeed Dean barge fleet. Their similarity is to be expected, built in consecutive years, 1887 and 1888, and with close Official Numbers, 94554 and 94559, both of 44 tons when built.

carried forty-two thousand ordinary stock bricks, which averaged one hundred tons in weight.

During my term of imprisonment aboard the *Bessie*, there was about a dozen of us barges arrived home from London together, some loaded with one thing and some with another. With this number of barges arriving at once there would be a couple of us mates that would go to the Foreman's house for every barge's orders. This always had to be done, night or day, and a mile or so to walk, no matter how long one had been at work beforehand. You never had to be tired; if one did get tired you had to work it off, irrespective of weather conditions you'd been through and so on, until the voyage's tasks were ended. So, just as me and another mate are about to land at one of our firm's wharves, known as the Lower Berth, to make our way to the Foreman's house, one of the hufflers[12] was rowing up the Creek and shouted "The *Fred*[13] is coming along loaded with gas breeze[14]. Will you get her orders?" We hadn't seen the *Fred* amongst us as we came down from London and how the mistake came about one never knew. Anyway, we got the Fred's orders and orders for all the other barges and passed them on to those concerned, and got the 'medals' one receives for doing someone else's work as well as one's own. But the *Fred* never arrived.

We are all berthed at our respective places ready for unloading, but not the *Fred*. Like all the other Mates, I go home and get turned in during the early hours of the morning for a few hours sleep, dreaming of the problems in store and imagining the Manager, Mr. George Andrews, awaiting his opportunity to pounce on me. And so it's down to the Office in the morning, in good time for nine o' clock to get our duties. And when the time arrived he flew out of the Office all hot and bothered, as we stood there. "Who got the Fred's orders last night?" Mr. George Andrews roared. "I did, sir." "Who told you the *Fred* was home?" "One of the hufflers, sir." "What huffler?" "Don't know, sir." "Who told you the *Fred* had got gas breeze in?" "Same huffler, sir." "And you don't know what huffler it was?" "No, sir." "Well, you keep yer tongue between yer teeth in future. I sent men, horses and carts this morning and no barge there. Who's going to pay 'em?" I had no answer. "If I find out who it was, he'll pay the penalty, and you," he said to me, "get back down aboard of yer barge." Mr. George was a smart chap but I don't think he ever found out who had given me the false information.

Smeed Dean's *Gore Court* and *Fred* with gear lowered (right), load under the rubbish chute by the Old Kent Road on the Grand Surrey Canal.

It was a very small percentage of the Mates that stayed with the same skipper for a few years. I'm trying to get another berth and in so doing, because my skipper found out, I got the sack. It was nothing unusual for this old chap to do, because I learned he had thirteen Mates in one year! If he could have snored twice with one breath while he was asleep to have annoyed someone, he would have got up and made a cup of tea to celebrate it!

---

[12] Huffler, possibly from the Dutch 'Hoveller'; a pilot with local knowledge who would come out to vessels navigating such as bridges and tortuous creeks to assist and advise.
[13] *Fred* of Rochester, built Murston 1881, 44 tons. - See APPENDIX A.
[14] Gas breeze: Ash produced by burning coal at gas works, breeze a synonym for ash.

CHAPTER IV CAPTAIN'S WAGES

In a day or so I am standing outside of the firm's Office, which was situated near the wharves where the skippers always gathered for their orders. Knowing the boys as they did, all the warmth went out to me for what had happened. Most of them were interested in this sort of thing, particularly when one got dislodged uncalled for, and many were ready to assist where they could. But like a spark out of the fire, our Manager, Mr. George Andrews, shrewd man as he was, and one who knew the breadth and depth of the smallest occurrence from one end of the estate to the other, stepped out of the Office door with his eyes scanning the men. He called to me "Winn, where's your barge." "Gone away, sir." "Why aren't you gone?" "Got the sack, sir." He stood for a moment motionless, with his brain working like the Scottish Express, and turned on his heel and said "Make haste and get another berth." and went back into the Office. I was sure I was still on his mind, and of us boys, me and the others, he was always foremost to assist the fatherless.

The huffler's boat is towed astern of the barge's boat as the huffler prepares to assist the crew to lower the gear and 'shoot' the King's Ferry Bridge. When the first railway crossing to the Isle of Sheppey was opened, the barges had priority over the train service, but that was soon changed, so the services of a huffler and 'lowering down' became the norm.

After a day or two I secured a boat and went down to Kings Ferry Bridge as a huffler, to assist the barges with their gear, lowering down, shooting the bridge and heaving up their rigging. This only lasted for a short time, then I was sent for, the message was "You are to go to the Office and see the Manager, Mr. George. He wants to speak to you." I went as instructed, "Good morning, Winn." "Good morning, sir." "I want you," he went on, "to take the *Perseverance*[1] away; her Captain has fell sick. Do you think you can do that?" "Yes, rather, sir." "Very well then, here's your Bill of Lading. You are bound to Wandsworth Gas Works with 40,000 of dark stock bricks."

And so I proceeded on the voyage with the *Perseverance* to Wandsworth, in command, able to afford a decent cloth pair of trousers at last, and a Mate under me to do most of the work. In a day or so I arrived there all safe and sound, discharged the bricks

[1] *Perseverance* of Rochester, built London 1824, 40 tons. - See APPENDIX A.

and loaded a back cargo of refuse from Lambeth Vestry Wharf, and was safely back home within a week. I took my stand with the other skippers to go into the Office for my two freights pay, about £3.16s.0d. I thought the world had swung round in my favour, and it had, but it was soon to swing back again.

Three pounds sterling for Rosie and sixteen bob for me meant something. We wasn't used to being loaded with money, but she knew what a shilling was worth. After we got over the shock and was ourselves again, we had a walk up the High Street, nodding to people now and again, with my bowler hat cocked a little.

But the novelty of being skipper had to die for the time being, because the Captain of the *Perseverance* got better, but the flowers in the jam jar that stood on what was our combined kitchen and dining and sitting room table always bloomed, and what a mansion it was to us. There was no thought of looking anywhere else for a job, as there was always someone needed in our firm, as we called it. As my dear old mother used to say "A rolling stone gathers no moss." But that's all right only in a way and calls for some argument. Then it's a question as to who is right, and who is going to prove it but, God so willing, and seeing my ends met, I stuck to the old firm, which was more like a father and a family of children.

And I sleep, and I rise, with renewed courage, and go down amongst the bargemen and the beloved barges, where some wouldn't dare to tread, blazing with ambition but with no more foundation other than the goodwill of someone else, with my services thrown in. As I have perhaps mentioned, our profession was no mug's game, unless we were all mugs and the sane people wouldn't do it. If they would, they couldn't - please allow me. It was a hereditary profession and practically no one else could rise to efficiency at the Thames sailing barge game. I have seen a large number try to do it, but most have failed.

And so, after a few mornings, I'm cruising around about headquarters, with the Office machinery at work and the Manager, Mr. George Andrews, had sent for me to see him at the Office. "Now, what are you going to do, Winn?" "Get another berth as soon as I can, sir." "Well, you go down to the shipyard to work, under Mr. Joe Ost, the yard Foreman, and you will be paid Captain's wages of £1 per week, until something comes along." "Thank you, sir." Of course, one didn't have to lose any time or one wouldn't get that amount, but almost anything was better than being Mate of the *Bessie*. Neither did it matter whether you were skipper, or what you was, there was none of you're getting to work at 8 a.m., you had to be in the yard at 6 a.m. sharp. One half-minute late and your £1 was reduced to nineteen shillings and four pence and no argument. Whatever the undertaking, the amount of work you got done wasn't taken into consideration.

It was all pretty decent for me, as well as being well pleased with the favoured consideration. Well, this Captain's job in the bargeyard only lasted about two months, with more or less every night at home in bed. That was a very strange thing to me, and it begun to get a little too regular as well. To some extent I saw it as the waste of one's life and the lowering of one's activity, and I began to miss my routine afloat very much. The three or four hours sleep was the far better game, and the best doctor I ever had but, sometimes, now and again, even a Mate's job afloat began to drag a little, but it had to be shaken off.

The Gov'nor, Mr. George Andrews, sent for me. I was up at the Office like a shot. I thought I was to go skipper again, for my sixteen bob from the *Perseverance* had long since disappeared. He said "Will you go away in the *Winnie*[2] for a voyage." I replied "But the Captain is a blackleg, sir." "I know," said he, "but will you oblige me?" I thought about my wife and our difficulties at home and said "Yes, sir." I was glad to get back to my old routine, where I could see the daybreak and face the storms. Of course, I knew the Captain well and he was quite a decent chap. Apart from his blacklegging he was certainly human.

But he wasn't a Thames Barge man, he was a coaster, and his name was William Sawyer. Working day and night I done the voyage to London and back to Sittingbourne with two cargoes in a week. The Captain fed the ship and charged me two shillings for my share, and I went bouncing home to Rosie with my voyage pay, thirty-four shillings, and not to be sneezed at in those days, irrespective of the time put in to earn it.

And so I stayed in the barge *Winnie* at the Captain's request, as in the circumstances nothing could be done to get me a skipper's berth, the only alternative a job in the Office. And with amicable give and take we got along very nicely. It lightened things up considerably for me and Rosie and we kept up a little better head of steam; more liberty and a freer hand, with more to get on with.

As you have understood, to be Mate in these barges wasn't all beer and skittles by a long chalk, but this berth was my first chance of anything like breathing space, with the years I was hanging about for promotion to Skipper. We worked together and become more like brothers than enemies, and some ten months passed in this way, and what a relief it was for me, as I kept watch

Mr. George Andrews, who became Managing Director in 1904 and shared the role with John H. Dean. John Dean was the son of George Hambrook Dean, who had become manager under George Smeed before the formation of Smeed Dean & Co. Ltd in 1875, when he became its Chairman. George Andrews was the son of John Andrews, who became a director after serving as brickworks' foreman in the 1870s.

[2] *Winnie* of Rochester, built Murston 1880, 45 tons. - See APPENDIX A.

Smeed Dean had a regular trade in bricks and brick rubble to Clacton, Essex, where the barges would unload into carts amongst the holiday-makers on the exposed beach where, from time to time they would get into trouble in strong onshore winds. The barge seen unloading in the photograph is Smeed Dean's *Victoria*.

for opportunities within our firm. We arrived home from a trip to Clacton and the Captain went to the Office as usual for the voyage's pay, and to my joy, he came to me and told me that the Gov'nor wanted to see me.

I went into the Office and see him. He looked at me and said "Good morning, Winn." "Good morning, sir." "Now, I've got a barge waiting already loaded for you to take charge of; it's the *William & Sarah*[3]." "Thank you, sir." "Will you take her?" "Yes sir, thank you." "Very well then," Mr. George read out the Riot Act, "We intend to have upright sober men; men who don't do damage, and men who don't lose time. I have been thinking about you for a long time and now your chance has come." 'I've been waiting for this.' I thought to myself. "You are bound to Old Kent Road, Surrey Canal, with thirty thousand of stock bricks, and make the best of your way." "Yes sir, Thank you."

It was certainly a day for rejoicing, although the *William & Sarah* was the worst old Packet we had in our fleet, known to us bargeman as the training ship. All young beginners had to go through

[3] *William & Sarah* of Faversham, built King's Arms Stairs, Surrey, 1838, 35 tons. - See APPENDIX A.

the mill in this way. When these promotions did come about, whether the old Packet had any bottom attached to her or not, Mr. George would treat the enrolment of young skippers, as though someone was being made Admiral of the battleship Hood. But it didn't do any harm in the long run and I was always grateful to him for what he done. I left the Office with my Bill of Lading, the long looked for document, all grins. I was then about twenty-three years of age.

I joined my old skipper for an hour or so before parting. It was more like losing an arm on either side to do this, but I had to get to business, with quite a bit to do in a short time. First it was home to Rosie, of course, to tell her the good news, and there was a bit of jollification in the kitchen to celebrate, then down to the good ship *William & Sarah*.

The first thing I noticed was that the pump was shipped. I unlocked the cabin and went down and had a look round, then had a look down the well hole - that's where you look to see if the ship has got any water in. I noticed she had got a little in the bilge, so I put a stick down the well hole for sounding purposes. I found she had water about a foot in depth. Blow me, I thought to myself, she sweats a bit! I pumped her out and made a dry ship of her for a little while. Worrying as it was, I had got my Bill of Lading in me pocket and I was Skipper, that's all that mattered. Rosie was home preparing something for tea, which was not to be missed if one had time to go home to get it.

As a boy of about 14 years of age I was briefly Mate in this old Packet, so we were not exactly strangers. In a couple of days I left Adelaide Dock, Sittingbourne with a young Mate with me, about sixteen years of age. *William & Sarah* was a little seventy tonner stumpy, old fashioned tiller, known as a rib-bender, which was well named; with a two inch steering line it was nothing new to have raw ribs with these weapons. But I was born with them and knew all their tricks. As you have read, for some years I had been Mate of our smart barges, and the *William & Sarah* had to do as she was told. We shuffled along up the dear old Thames once again, but me as permanent Captain this time, and eventually arrived at the Surrey Canal and the Old Kent Road, were we was towed by a horse belonging to a Mr. Biggs. Mr. Biggs was, in those days, known as the Surrey Canal Cut Ranger, employed by the Surrey Commercial Dock Company, and a very fine fellow he was to us bargemen. But look out if he had to tell you a second time to do, or not to do, something. Let me say Mr. Biggs was admired by all for his frankness!

And so I'm ashore in a brace of shakes to see the builder, or the consignee of the bricks, and back again on board as soon as possible to get up the rigging ready for work, the discharging of our cargo of bricks. Of course, I had in mind the old Surrey Music Hall for the evenings programme, not forgetting the little fortune I had got to come for my two freights on my arrival home, where the other half of my pleasure would be anxiously awaiting to receive her new skipper. And

Bricks were loaded in the Adelaide Dock, part of the Murston premises where Smeed Dean had both brick and cement works, and where flints from the company's pits were taken for shipment.

so the happy days had well started for fate to decide. I loaded refuse at Camberwell Vestry and so passed out of the Canal and arrived home in a few days. "Well," Mr. George said, "you've got back safe, Captain Winn." "Yes sir." "How do you find the old barge?" "She makes a drop of water, sir." "Yes, I know she does, do your best with her, you'll have the next shift that comes along."

With new enthusiasm and hopes, the wheels of fortune had begun to turn in a different direction and I was determined to rise in my profession - and when being addressed by Mr. George Andrews as Captain Winn, instead of just Winn, can you wonder at bargemen rising to such heights as they did. For me it meant casting off the old flap trousers and donning new ones with side pockets and fly fronts, such was the honour so suddenly bestowed upon me as Captain, and sometimes even washing oneself every day.

We all took seriously the responsibility that came with this honour. There were many of us, and it was a grand sight for the onlooker to watch the barges sailing about together and manoeuvring to see who could gain a length on the other, for we was always racing, which was a lifetime study. Oft times the barges would foul each other while tacking about in close quarters. Some would laugh, others couldn't hardly see what was funny about it, and if there were half a minute to spare, the one who thought he was right would jump aboard of the other and shake his fist in the Captain's face, and I have known them to connect on occasions.

Most bargemen were known for their alertness and, if you'll allow me to say, it's a nerve-wracking profession, but to take them as a whole they were a noble crowd. I have known barge Captains to go mad because they could always beat the other fellow and others come to the same fate because they was always behind, and others went mad because they could never rise to the proficiency needed for command.

Some of these spritty barges was that aged, and made enough water that would drown ducks, let alone carry a dry cargo, and I shall be telling you more about that later on.

And so with the goodwill of Mr. G. Andrews, the Manager, I blowed about up and down the dear old Thames, in every creek, dock, canal, and at near enough every wharf there, and my first eleven months quickly passed in the training ship as skipper, as happy as a sand boy, as the saying goes.

One of the incidents that happened during this time was when I was navigating Vauxhall Bridge under oars. I got a little bit out of the set of the tide. One had only to be a couple of feet adrift, then it was look out for the fireworks. I dropped anchor to save the barge striking the bridge, but we swung around and the end of the sprit caught the bridge and broke.

This kind of error in our firm was a serious mistake and, for certain, a carpet court-martial for me when I arrived home. Because these sprits were huge and expensive spars, fifty odd feet long and roughly ten inches diameter, I had to stir up surplus courage to face the beak when I went into the Office to draw the freightage. At the Office, by the look of things, I think the Manager was waiting for me. He was looking down at his desk and didn't say anything for a moment. Presently he looked up and roared "So you have broke your sprit." "Yes, sir." "How?" he

asked. "Well, sir…" "It's not well." he retorted. "How did you break it?" "I was about to shoot Vauxhall Bridge, sir, and I could see it was doubtful whether I should clear, so I dropped my anchor to save hitting the bridge and she swung around and the sprit caught the bridge." "Then why didn't you let go your anchor sooner?" "Because I thought she'd clear sir, until I let go." "You thought?" said he, "Yes sir, you pay me to think." "We don't pay you to break sprits." he shouted, throwing the pencil on the desk, his bowler on the back of his head and him all hot and smoking.

Vauxhall Bridge was opened on 4th June 1816 and comprised nine arches of 78 feet span. Despite the arch width, the bridge was a constant problem for navigation. The tolls never recovered the £250,000+ build cost, and it was replaced with a five arch bridge in 1898.

He disappeared into the inner Office. My braces were slipping in my sweat. He came back out and I was wondering what was going to happen. I didn't know whether he was going to sack me, or kiss me. He looked at me, I looked at him. He got a book down and started to write in it, tearing the page out and passing it to me. It was an order made out to the shipyard for a new sprit. "And think sooner next time." "Yes sir." and I hadn't a dry thread on me, such was the discipline in 1892.

Smeed Dean's little stumpy *Alfred* is at Putney, unloading her cargo into a horse-drawn cart.

At the end of the eleven months there came a shift around amongst the barges. One of the skippers got the sack out of a little stumpy barge called the *Alfred*[4]. She was a nice little toy of a barge, with a steering wheel fitted in place of her tiller, which was much admired. So I had high hopes, but the Gov'nor hadn't said anything about the man getting the sack out of the *Alfred* to me. I waited until the next day to see if Mr. George Andrews was going to give me the shift, but he didn't. So I got up enough steam to walk into the Office and ask if I could see him, and out he come. I said "Pardon, sir, I hear the barge *Alfred's* vacant." "Who said so?" he replied. "The Captain told me so. He told me he has got the sack." "He has." the Gov'nor said. "Then can I have the *Alfred* sir?" "No. I'm afraid you can't." he said, so I reminded him that when I took charge of the *William & Sarah* he had promised that I should have the next shift. I told him that out of my last eleven months in the *William & Sarah* I had spent ten of them pumping. "Well," he said, "I'm sorry Captain, but one of our senior Captains wants the *Alfred*, one who we thought never would have shifted. He has been in the *Kent*[5] for twenty years. Will you take the *Kent*?" "Yes sir." I replied with enthusiasm. "Very well then, you and Captain Mantle arrange it between you."

He had evidently forgiven or forgotten about my broken sprit and I was glad to take charge of the *Kent*. She didn't suffer so much with the pumping, though there was times when one had to stick some of these noble craft ashore on the mud to give them what

[4] *Alfred* of London, built Bankside, 1847, 33 tons. - See APPENDIX A.
[5] *Kent* of Faversham, built Sittingbourne, 1860, 35 tons. - See APPENDIX A.

is known in the old sailing barge line as a Blackwall caulk. That is for the mud to enter the cracks were the water runs in, and when she refloated you would have a brand new ship until, of course, such times when the mud washed out again. So me and Captain Mantle met and talked over our new roles, as bargemen do, and of the qualifications of the craft he was about to leave. When bargemen got a shift, 'If you find a bed bug or two, old man.' one would say to the other, 'don't shout it about. I can assure you she ain't got many in her and you'll find her nice and clean otherwise.' But one didn't take much notice of these comments, whether it was a bed bug, a mouse, or a rat, because the good ship *William & Sarah* that I am just leaving was like a small zoo in that regard.

You should have seen the Gov'nor's proud eyes all aglow when he was about to announce these shifts from one barge to another, thinking as he did that he had got so many men efficient for their task with these craft. He knew that muscles like cannonballs were needed, even if there was nothing to do but pump!

These shift days made a change from the ordinary routine, and if landsmen were to see it they would think that Drake had just arrived home at Plymouth from the Spanish Armada. But Mr. George was our hope, and we stuck to him like bees to a hive. We were proud of our spritty barges, although one never knew, one day from another, whether she would float or sink. Some of these dear old packets was a bit ancient and needed a bit of watching. Of course we always had these old craft for young beginners to practice on, to break them in properly. There was no doubt about it, and as you read on you'll see that a bargeman's life was well worth living and that in many cases humour played a great part in the sailing barge way of life.

A small stumpy barge negotiates the bascule bridge which carried the Becton Tramway across Barking Creek.

And so I have taken over as Captain of the *Kent* and must now go home and break the news to Rosie. No doubt we will have a bit of jollification over the strides I'm making with my new undertaking as skipper, and another 2/6d. extra to draw when I had done a round trip to London and back. 2/6d. in those days was a lot of money, another shilling would almost fit the ship out with one's sea stock of food, and within two days of the change-over I was underway yet again bound for Charlston's Wharf, Barking Creek.

Barking was a noted spot for us bargemen, because

one could get a big smoked haddock for a penny ha'penny, or a big basin of stewed eels for tuppence, or bloaters, eight for sixpence. And there was the two pound loaf for just tuppence farthing, so you see, only as far back as 1892 one could get food almost just for the asking. Messrs. Hewett Fishing Company Limited's trawlers all went to make Barking what it was, a very busy place. Another big business was the jute factory with seven or eight hundred girls working there. Bargemen were quite at home in Barking and the old water-worked flourmill was another spectacle there, and on the whole it was quite a picturesque place.

And so I sailed up and down the old Thames in the little spritty sailing barge *Kent* for about 17 months, getting in trouble and getting out again, but less pumping. Me and the *Kent* became great pals because she was reasonable in her drinking habits! When one has to turn out in the small hours of the morning and attend to barges because they make so much water, things are not so pleasant. It is anything but comfortable when riding[6]; off and on one is in and out of your bunk to see what water she is making and there's but very little sleep to be had. That disturbance incurs extra strain than you otherwise would have if your barge had lay peacefully quiet, and not taking water. But as long as one is Captain, young and strong, you didn't take too much notice of her troubles and infirmities. As you have heard, we had our remedies as well as our troubles with leaky craft. If she come off too sick, we would stick her on the mud and close her up for a while. That was the only way to get a quiet night or two until she started her old tricks again.

On the other hand, one had the pleasure as well as the work, to have them tight, and their clothes spick and span. With taut sheets and a blow, one could have some fun with them, the drawers sliding about the cabin floor, you could almost blow them bottom up. But not an eggcup full of water did some of them make, that was something worth knowing when on the wheel. They were jolly good craft, chaps, jolly good craft - I have seen them lay down to such an angle in a squall that one could almost tar their bottoms, doing almost everything but turning over. One could handle some of them like a baby and they would answer their helm like lightning, almost as sensitive as a horse and its driver.

I had one once, she'd lie down if one only looked at her with a moderate breeze, meaning in the nautical world that she was crank, or in other words, tender. Similar to people, there was hardly two alike, and there were thousands of these red sailed graceful ladies. But then they were not all red sails. Lee's fleet of barges in the Medway were all black sails, Lloyd's Paper Mill

---

[6] Riding: A seafarer's term for being at anchor, hence Riding Light hoist at night when anchored as a warning to other vessels.

barges were yellow sails, just three of them, namely the *Alice Lloyd*, *Frank Lloyd*, and *Annie Lloyd*, and very smart barges they were, all sprit rigged with Lloyd's News painted in their sails. Occasionally you'd see one or two barges with a new suit of sails all white, which made a grand sight when they were mingled together with the other colours in the dear old Thames.

And, by the way, I don't hardly know how to describe these noble fellows, the Captain bargemen. For one thing they needed a flood of wits to be in the running, though I have known them get the sack because they had too much, and vice versa. One man once applied for a Captain's berth at one of the sailing barge firms and the owners were taxing him as to his qualifications. They asked him several questions, and one was whether he had ever hit any of the

Thames bridges and the Captain said "No, sir." "Well," the owner said, "I'm afraid you won't be much use to us, because if ever you do hit one, you won't know how to get clear." That was a nasty atmosphere to be in, because we all wanted to live, and another poor chap who had hit one of the Thames bridges, admitted to it and lost the berth on account of it!

It was Vauxhall Bridge, the old Vauxhall Bridge which had nine arches to span the River Thames and a very dangerous bridge it was. It has been hit by craft more times than any other bridge between the Tower Bridge and Windsor, and placed in the awkwardest part of the Thames it was very difficult to navigate under oars. I have known, when shooting Vauxhall Bridge on a spring tide ebb and fresh water down, a drop, or an overfall to be correct, of two feet, owing to the tide rushing through these arches. This bridge was made of stone, and by hitting it one poor unfortunate skipper knocked off one of his leeboards and lost it. So

Passing through the London bridges under oars was a highly skilled task. The wind and tide were never the same twice, and the characteristic eddies around the bridge piers were always ready to catch the unwary. Here a barge negotiates a side arch of the 1869 Blackfriars bridge, the span width 170 feet. Vauxhall Bridge spans were just 78 feet wide.

he approached an underwaterman, and they were plentiful in those days, and they were clever too with their hooks, to get the leeboard back if he could. The skipper approached his owners and told them what had happened and they commended him for what he had done in the matter. In a day or so the underwaterman dragged up the leeboard and took it to the barge and charged the skipper thirty shillings, which he paid. The Captain was well satisfied and eventually saw his owners and told them he had got his leeboard back again, thinking he was going to get his money back. The owner said "Well done, Captain, you're the sort of man we want, with experience, and I wish you the best of luck next time you shoot the bridge." The skipper said "Thank you sir, but I've paid thirty shillings for it sir." "Yes," the owner said, "you got off light. I can see they have got a job on to twist you - and a bit of luck you didn't knock the other one off!"

Vauxhall Bridge was a terror and, as you have heard, was no mugs game if one was to succeed. Now those leeboards are made of large pieces of oak planks fastened together with convex iron bands and rivets, some of them weigh half a ton and more and in size, according to the size of the barge. They are of fan shape, and which answer when lowered to prevent leeway in these flat bottom barges. Without them it's almost impossible to handle these craft when sailing.

So one fine glorious morning I arrived home at Sittingbourne from the last voyage in the little barge *Kent*. I am about to make another shift into a little bigger barge. The birds were singing and the caulking mallets ringing at the shipyard, and me as happy as a sandboy presented with heaven on earth. There was plenty of trade to look forward to and for me a flood of expectations and not a worry in the world, 25 years of age and time flying like a kite. We moored at one of the wharves, and the men were waiting to discharge the cargo. I went up to the Office for my freightage money and to meet the Gov'nor once again, Mr. George. "Good morning, Captain." "Good morning, sir." "I've got the *Florence*[7] here waiting for you, topsail barge and a wheel, just what you want, and don't blow her over." "Thank you sir, I won't if I can help it." "Four thousand bricks larger than the *Kent* and ten shillings more on the down cargo from London, she'll suit you down to the ground." "Yes sir, thank you, sir." But this is how the ten shillings worked out; the owners took five of the ten shillings, I had three shillings and fourpence, and the Mate of the *Florence* had one shilling and eight pence, that's what the Gov'nor called ten shillings more on the down cargo. It really didn't take any of us long to reckon it up, but I assure you it was appreciated, and Rosie well knew the difference and value of the extra 3/4d. For me, presently, it meant an extra tin of boot polish and a new bowler hat.

---

[7] *Florence* of Faversham, built Murston, 1858, 39 tons. - See APPENDIX A.

How pleased Mr. George was to think that he had raised the most tiresome boy he had under him to such a height. Happy days, and he had the patience of Job, and he needed it! "You are bound to Crabtree Dock, Fulham." Crabtree Dock is a place about halfway between Putney Bridge and Hammersmith were the big old crabtree stood and grew many years before I was born. And there was a public house there, named The Crabtree Inn[8], and a very busy place it was on Sundays, in particular. When I was a boy with my Father, me and Bill, my brother, picked up many shillings there minding pleasure skiffs, and on Oxford and Cambridge Boat Race days father picked up a few pounds by letting people come on our barge to view the race, and that was a Godsend to us then. People used to visit this spot because of its ancient name and it still rings in my ears as well.

Extending a five year winning streak, the Oxford crew approach the finish of the 1895 University Boat Race.

And so *Florence* is the next consideration. She too was getting on in life, but she was alright and I'd known her many years; a nice little thing for a young man to practice on, very handy, and a practical man could almost thread her through the eye of a needle. When empty and in a high wind, she wasn't particular in showing part of her bottom, and young, strong, robust men was just in their element when their barges would sail like this.

The time had long since arrived when me and Rosie wanted for very little, but it's a very fine thing to have to go without something what one wants and can't get. Then things are so much more appreciated when you are able to get them, and much greater valued than if you had it straight away, and you are the more

---

[8] It was not a 'big old crabtree' that stood in the grounds of the Crabtree Inn, but an enormous and ancient weeping willow, with branches trained into arbours with seats and tables underneath. The inn's name came from the crab-apple orchards of Crabtree Farm nearby. The Inn was demolished in 1898, but there is still a pub of that name on the waterfront.

contented people of the two. Small privileges were put in my way by the Manager to earn more money and being in the background awaiting a decent command any longer was all forgotten.

In the spring of 1894 I was at a wharf at Wandsworth almost touching Wandsworth Bridge. It was on the Sunday of the University Boat Race, morning time, a hard bright sunny morning and a very hard westerly wind blowing. I was on deck and heard some one shouting with all their might. I looked out into the river and there saw a skiff full of water. It was a coxed four to be correct, and all the occupants were in the water, five men in number.

I jumped into my small boat and was out to them in a brace of shakes. It was some kind of a novelty to see these chaps, although they were all afraid and gasping out a mournful cry "Ho, save me skipper, save me skipper." and I'll wager every one of them would have given a hundred pounds to get out of the water while he was in it. I kept on saying "That's all right boys, you're all right, you keep quiet, I'll soon have you out." but I could see and hear that they wasn't thinking so, but eventually I got the five of them in my boat and put them on the shore near Wandsworth Gas Works. Then up the river I went after their skiff, nice mahogany made, and it belonged to a Mr. Gus Brewer at the Star and Garter Hotel, Putney. He also had a boathouse near where my barge was at Wandsworth, where I took the skiff after I picked her up, and handed her over to young Mr. Brewer.

A very large St. George's flag flies over the Star & Garter Hotel at Putney. Mr. Brewer's skiff raft is seen just below the walkway span to the floating pontoon. The little stumpy barge unloads her cargo into carts on the foreshore, no doubt keen to finish before the flood tide reaches them.

As luck would have it, I had no sooner done this than an eight oar skiff swamped opposite the Gas Works. This boat was 60 feet 6 inches long and also belonged to Mr. Gus Brewer, eight gentlemen in her and the cox. These gentlemen kept their seats with the exception of the cox. He jumped overboard and that was something like seamanship, and they got in my boat, one by one, and I landed them on shore, of course. This life saving business has taken some time one way and the other. Of course, this sort of thing is part and parcel of our profession and is unavoidable in the circumstances. Presently I heard someone shouting, but it wasn't a swamped boat this time. It was the five men from the first boat that I had picked up. I was still in my boat. "Skipper," they were shouting, "come on ashore, we want to pay you." I shouted back to them "That's quite alright boys, that's quite alright."

But there was no pacifying them and I felt I had to go ashore. They were all drunk, and you can imagine, with the fair in full swing there were scores of people there, some kissing me, others nearly choking me, and "What a man." says they, and they are dancing all around. "Come on, boy, what yer goner have?" By the time they were done with me I was half drunk with the fumes from them. "He's a jolly good fellow and we're agoin' to pay yer." And with a few more fumes for myself I said "Now that's quite alright boys, I know your feelings, but I'm a teetotaller and I'm as pleased as you are that I was about and on the spot to help you."

But it was no good, some brought beer and some lemonade and someone gave me two cigars, and I was surrounded like a rat in a trap. Presently someone popped up and said "Ere y'are, me old brother, take this." Well, you know what these Cockney sportsmen are; it's do or die. I didn't want to be seen in this sort of thing, but the 'Circus' was still in progress. Someone had a tin whistle and I pleaded with them to let me go. And eventually one of the five survivors slipped a half a crown in my hand and nearly squeezed me to death with joy. They will not take no for an answer, I was all day at this function and missed my hot dinner. But no lives were lost and that's all that mattered, but the eight-oar boat broke up into pieces before I could get her under control, but I secured the eight oars and the rudder. I was warmly congratulated by these gentlemen, and Mr. Brewer, and was handed a splendid present in real money. But the old half crown, yer know, that was squeezed into my hand, floated on top of the water! Some of us knew what these Cockney boys were, and no doubt none of them ever for got that Sunday. But this was only a sideline of one's life programme, pleasure with work, disaster and joy.

And after a deep and peaceful night's sleep, Monday arrived and the lightermen came to unload my cargo of bricks. These men came from all parts of London and were better known as 'Bricks', but this mob, as they are called, were locals and as soon as

I showed my self the cheery cheeky call rang out "Good morning, sailorman." "Morning boys." I replied. "I'll bet you're alright for a couple of fivers." We had to answer them back now and then, in case they thought we didn't hear them. These lightermen knew the English language from A to Z and could speak it fluently. Our owners were religious and didn't approve of us arguing with anyone, although it was some forty miles or more from Sittingbourne to the Upper Thames, and the mice did pretty much as they liked when the cats wasn't about.

Now there were several grades of these lightermen. Concerning their apprenticeship, there were two years, five years and seven years men. The seven years man could do anything on the Thames to get a living, the five years man not so many privileges and the two years man even less, he only allowed to work on lighters, tugs, or any heavy cargo craft, but not allowed to 'scull'. This was anywhere above Gravesend, and some of these

Clear to all were the undoubted skills of the Thames lightermen, working their magic in the London River, once so crowded you could often see more craft than water.

men were quite youngsters and hardly knew whether the tide was setting south or north until they hit a bridge - then they would go home wiser. But when we chipped at them about their mistakes we soon found out they knew everything else and sometimes we gained knowledge which all went to balance things, as well as to brighten one up a little. It's surprising what one can learn out of other people's mistakes; I think the Lighterage and Sailing Barge School was rather ahead of Oxford and Cambridge University.

And so summer followed the spring of 1894 and the Wandsworth eight-oar and coxed-four boat disasters. During one of my voyages from Sittingbourne I was berthed at Swan Wharf, Fulham, near Putney Bridge. It was flood tide and I was sitting aft on my barge playing a concertina, gazing around, when I noticed a boat sailing up stream. She was passing through the arch nearest to me when she caught a strong squall and over she went. There were two men in her and, appropriately her name was the *Storm*. I put down my concertina and jumped in my boat and got to them in a quick time, but not soon enough.

I saved one man, and the other, his pal, sank out of sight. Of course, there were others who saw this from Putney side of the river and boats were putting out from all directions to go to their assistance. Dragging was taking place instantly and this man was dragged up and placed on a raft opposite the Star and Garter at

Putney. All this was managed within half an hour of the capsizing of the boat and he still had life in him. There was a doctor on the scene instantly, pumping in progress and nothing lacking in the way of science, for two hours. I regret to tell you it was just too late to save his life, although life was briefly produced during the struggle. And so with a sad ending, as well as warm congratulations for my efforts, I returned to my barge to get on with the race of life, a little different than the race for life I had just done. I spared a thought for the other fellow who survived; he wasn't quite so fortunate as myself, and if the rest of the people could realize what it meant to live, for the other chap, despite the loss of his pal, they wouldn't want the doctor so often.

During the next day, while loading refuse here, the dustmen wanted to know all about it - that's dear old London all over isn't it?

"Who was it, skipper?" and "How did it happen?" and "Well done, skipper." and the rest of it, which I took with all good part. And again I put this all aside, with new courage and renewed thoughts and new ideas, to get on with my job. We finished loading and eventually arrived home at Sittingbourne. With the usual grooming, of course, a light blue jersey, with black doe-skin jacket and trousers to match, and the never forsaken bowler hat, and it was down to the Office as usual for my pay and orders, and for the honour of having to do this as a routine. This all played a great part in my life, with our Mr. G. Andrews, our Manager, at the head of all our affairs, and there wasn't much done that slipped his notice.

While he was paying me he said "What have you been up to this trip?" "Nothing that I know of, sir." I replied. "Did you save

The Smeed Dean wharves at Murston, the barge-building shed to the right, a retired barge in the process of being dismantled in the foreground. To the left of the photo is the Brickmakers Arms, a popular haunt for many Smeed Dean workers, though not for George Winn, a teetotaller at heart.

a man's life at Putney?" "Yes sir." That was a relief, as I had thought for a moment I was for it again. He asked me how it happened and I told him the story. "It puzzles me," he went on, "that you always seem to be on the spot." "When did you know, sir?" "I knew of it the next day, and if you don't take care, it will happen to you." I done a grin, "That's all right sir, I've been over a time or two." "I'd rather you than me." said Mr. George. "Boat sailing's good fun, sir." "Seems like it!" said he.

And so I carry on with *Florence*, just a little toy of a barge, and enjoy the glorious fun I could get out of her when sailing, and without turning out at night to see what water she'd made. What a relief it was for a young skipper after more or less being married to craft very near all holes and cracks. And to get the wind on your stern, believe me, it was a great asset, especially for the Mate because he had to bear the brunt when there was a stiff foul wind. I have known them to be knocked out, but ever they rose again to their task. Yes, readers, the proof of the duff's in the eating, it was Rule Britannia with these Thames red sail spritty bargemen. 'Nelson Fashion', at peace or war, give her her bonnet[9], and you could do what you liked with her. Once you had to take that off her, she'd lie down and wouldn't do anything. That is one of the things one has to dig out by experience. It's just

With the passage of time, barges increased in size, needing bigger rudders, which needed bigger tillers, arguably making them even more dangerous.

doubtful whether the best of the sailormen ever got all the tricks out of these craft, what they had in them, but from a nautical point of view I have seen some marvellous things done with them. But with all *Florence's* good deeds, I've seen the times when she could kick as well as run in her 'tiller' days. Discarding the tiller didn't steer one clear of danger, although a grand improvement the steering wheel is.

---

[9] Bonnet: Originally an extra sail fastened to the foot of a square sail; in this context probably any sail additional to the working sailplan.

CHAPTER V   WAIT OUTSIDE THE OFFICE, CAPTAIN

While underway, with a hard wind and a choppy sea, one must know whether the wheel is going to fly to the steersman or from him. It can be easily misjudged with lack of experience and many men have been thrown over the top of the wheel in that way, getting a bad hurt to the shoulder or arm, or one eye banged up, and likely enough all three. But no medals for the pain, of course, it's all in the programme. Just getting one eye banged up, there wasn't much notice taken, so long as there wasn't any bones broken as well.

I will never forget an incident that befell the *Florence* when she had a tiller and was skippered by a Captain George Simmons. It was one hard winter in 1895; the River Thames was frozen over as far down as Woolwich, the East and West River Swale was also frozen over, and about 40 of our spritty barges were moored at the wharves in Milton Creek at Sittingbourne. That's when I first

skated, but it took me some little while to learn, as a lot of my time was occupied standing still, having a rest, and getting used to the ice coming up, now and again, and hitting me on the back of the head! After about five weeks the hard weather broke and we all set sail for London. But even then we couldn't navigate King's Ferry Bridge owing to ice, so had to go round the East end of the Isle of Sheppey. Although it was much further for us, it had to be faced.

1895, Tower Bridge, just a year old, is shrouded in freezing mist, the icy Thames frozen over.

The River Swale at King's Ferry Bridge in the great frost of 1895, navigation impossible as the ice reached from the mainland to the Isle of Sheppey.

I was in the *Kent* and Captain George Simmons in the *Florence*, both with tillers. We were both bound to the Cory's coal derrick, Charlton, to load coal for Messrs. Lloyds Paper Mills, Milton, Nr. Sittingbourne, and we decided to chum together for the voyage. We both got our cargo of coal, and we had to take the same route back and pass round the East end of the island. While tacking up the part of the Swale known as the East Grounds we were very close to each other and there was not much room to play in.

I was dangerously close to the *Florence's* stern and her skipper shouted "Where are you coming to?" and still sticking to his tiller looking aft at me. And I'm all hot and bothered and a freak squall blowing, and me doing my utmost to keep clear. But I collided with his rudder and the tiller swung against hit him and

Barges lie hemmed in by ice in the creeks of the Swale. When the thaw comes, the ice floes can inflict serious damage to the barges' hulls. Planks or timber baulks were used as fenders between the ice and hull planking.

knocked poor George Simmons flying overboard into the icy water. It makes you laugh looking back, but it wasn't funny at the time. His Mate threw him a lifebuoy and I jumped in my dinghy and picked him up and got him back aboard, Both barges were together on the mud with their sails flogging like a couple of swans in a typhoon.

We got the skipper down the cabin and trimmed him up. It was a nasty blow, but no bones broken that we could find and no bloodshed, but he looked a bit seedy and he said he felt seedy. We'd usually got some remedies on board; cough mixture, paregoric tablets, Dutch drops[1], and oftimes, snuff, in case of accidents, though there were many barges around which hadn't got them and would go about unthinkingly or careless as one might say. So we made George Simmons comfortable in the bunk and set about getting the sails stood up and getting the barges in a proper anchorage for the night, before telling the skipper he would be better in the morning.

I dozed about the greater part of the night with him and by the time it was breakfast, I felt about half-cooked myself. So the unfortunate skipper turned out, but he didn't look too fit and said he was as stiff as a plank, but will-power played its part and we both got underway and were shortly at our wharves in Milton Creek. The skip, George Simmons, was much better after a little exercise and was soon off home.

The next morning I've got to walk the carpet for certain. I knew that the night before to be correct. George lived close to me and we walked down to the Office together. I said "You go in the Office before me." though he looked a bit shaky "and make it as good as you can for me, boy." In he went. I knew whatever he said it wouldn't help me much, because the Gov'nor was always right. George Simmons came out and made over to see me, while someone else nipped in, but the Gov'nor sent him out again and called out for me. In I went. "How many tons of coal have you got in?" was his opening words. "Seventy-two, sir." He hadn't looked at me yet. He put the freight money on the desk and sat back in his chair while I picked it up.

I think he was looking at me; not a murmur, and I was thinking to myself 'Darn good, I may have got away with it' and was about to go out and as I glanced at him, he was looking at me with eyes like saucers and quite nasty. And out it came "Now what have you been up to, trying to sink the *Florence* as well as very near drowning her Captain?" "I'm very sorry, sir." "Don't talk to me with excuses - only two of you in the river and you deliberately sail head first into him; look at the man, half dead." "I've been looking at him

---

[1] Dutch Drops: Once a general tonic, appetite stimulant and diuretic based on oil of turpentine and sulphur, still available today, but only for equine applications!

all last night and done my best for him." I ventured. "Then why didn't you keep clear of him instead of knocking him overboard?" Mr. George jumped up out of the chair, still looking at me. "You be here at the Office tomorrow morning at eleven o'clock." I knew what that meant; walking the carpet and facing the directors to learn my fate, namely Mr. Hambrook Dean and Mr. John Andrews, our Manager's father, and he was a terror, a country born and bred man, who knew but very little grammar.

The next morning arrived and I'm at the Office when requested and was shown into the inner Office where the fun began. This was Mr. John Andrews' usual way when talking to his men in these kind of circumstances. "Well, mate," he roared out. "we've heard all about this serious calamity and fortunately for you, the man wasn't drowned. What have you got to say about it, mate?" I thought to myself for a moment, then said "Unavoidable, sir." I thought he was going to explode. "What do you mean, mate, 'unavoidable', unavoidable indeed. You wanted to be first and you didn't care how you done it, you could drown people and then say 'unavoidable'." "Yes sir." "Yes sir, mate" the old man repeated in a rage. Mr. Dean then broke in and said "Let him explain, John, if he can." "Yes sir." says I "Unavoidable. The *Florence* was faster than my barge and while turning up the Grounds he passed me and before he could get far enough ahead his barge smelt the mud, reducing her speed, and causing me to collide with his rudder. His tiller flew over taking the skipper with it, poor chap, and knocked him overboard and I saved him, thank you, sir. That's all."

He rung the bell and the office boy came. He said to the boy "Tell the Manager I want him." and he said to me "Wait outside the office, Captain." A quarter of an hour passed, seeming more like an hour. I was called in again and asked to sit down for the first time. "Well, mate," Mr. John quietly went on, "we are fully convinced that it was an unfortunate pure accident and I'm sorry you didn't explain in the first place." 'Some hopes.' I said to myself making quite sure he didn't hear me, or I should have stood an excellent chance of being hanged! He went on "We are also convinced, mate, if it wasn't for the likes of you, the man would have been drowned. That's all. You may go about your work." "Thank you, sir." As I was passing out of the Office the Manager shook hands with me, and the squall was over, but it was not to be the last.

As a result of this, getting steering wheels put in the tiller steered barges became a priority for Smeed Dean & Co. Ltd. Shortly after the accident the *Florence* was decorated with a steering wheel, while the same Captain still had charge of her, and many a joke was enjoyed afterwards over how it had come about.

Now you have heard something about these old 'Packets' as well as the good ones, and also what you have missed by not being born a bargeman. With the old packets it was as much like a museum as anything you can imagine. We had one really old dear still at work and getting on in years. She was called the *Elizabeth* and she was built at Aylesford, Kent in 1812, sprit rigged with topsail, and was swim headed, that is to say she had a head similar to a London lighter. What a lady; we all knew her, make no mistake about it, and she had got so weak in the joints that nobody wanted to skipper her.

When there was a shift about to be made, from one barge to another, you could always hear something amongst the bargemen as to their preferences. One would say "I don't want the old *Elizabeth*." "No," another would chime in, "he's (meaning the Gov'nor) no cause to think I'm going to pump the old bugger about night and day." "Maybe," someone else would butt in, "but don't forget she's a 110 tonner." "So she may be," the other fellow would say, "but I don't want the old cow." "Frightened to go to sleep on her." says Jack. "She has all the pick of the work, you know," someone says, "and she's been doing two freights a week." "Yes, and a freight of water to pump out as well." Nobby put in, "I'll take bloody good care she don't drown me." "Don't you believe it boy, you can be drowned without going in the *Elizabeth*. Poor old Jack Brunger was drowned while in charge of one of our small stumpy barges called the *Whitehall*[2]. Even taxi cab drivers get drowned[3]."

And so I'm about to end my time in the *Florence*. She was the size of barge one would have charge of before one was promoted into our smart 100 tonners, but that's where the snag come, for the *Elizabeth* was classed as a 100 tonner as well! So me and *Florence* had our ups and downs together for about nine months, and no regrets.

One fine day I was sailing home and arrived at King's Ferry Bridge and the huffler jumped on board to help with the gear. He was all smoke and fire with the joy of his job and anxious to tell me that the *Elizabeth*, laying at one of the wharves loaded, was waiting for me to take charge of her. "Who said so?" says I, " Everybody knows it, old man." He replied. "But how does the Gov'nor know I'll take her?" I asked. "Well, there it is old man, it's up to you." "Well, I hope the old bugger sinks through the mud before I get there." But she didn't, of course. So I arrived up the Creek and the Gov'nor was down on the wharf, shouting to me "Come up the Office, George, as soon as you get done." "Very good, sir, and I hope you have a fine day."

These smart 100 ton barges, known as the Forty-twoers for the 42,000 bricks they carried, were much coveted by the young

---

[2] *Whitehall* of Rochester, built Murston 1881, 37 tons. - See APPENDIX A.

[3] It was not unheard of for a London taxi horse to bolt in harness and drag the cab and driver to an untimely end in the Thames.

The crude swim head and budget stern barge was often a far less efficient hull to sail, but more easily and cheaply built. This construction had an inherent weakness where the flat bottom met the 'runs' fore and aft.

bargemen, as you have understood. Up to the Office I went and the Gov'nor was there waiting for me, "Well," he started, "since you've been away there's been a shift round in the barges, and the *Elizabeth's* vacant for you." "Thank you, sir, but I'd rather stay in the *Florence* if I stand my same chance for one of the 100 tonners." "I don't think you will." says he. I knew it was a waste of time arguing. "She's a task you know, sir, she's very old and makes a lot of water." I ventured "Yes, yes, I know she makes a drop of water at times." and all in one breath he added "She's got all good seven inch pumps in her." "Yes, I know she has, sir." "What we want as well is to try and find a remedy to stop it running in." He paused for a moment, "Yes," he said, "that's the trouble with the *Elizabeth*."

So I had to decide to skipper this old Packet. This was in 1896, and what a handful she was; no shape or make but, as it turned out, it was marvellous what she would do. Under her clouts[4], her bottom was all tingles and smothered with tar and hair, and her old ribs well decayed; some lady, I assure you. It was nothing unusual for her to make eighteen inches of water in one night, but it was mostly for Rosie's sake that I was to master this task for four years, and a real task it was.

But it was marvellous the speed one could get out of this old girl. Why it was I don't think anyone knew. She was weak and always making water, but although as old as she was, her well hole never dry, she was never behind in showing some of the smart ones a clean stern.

But what did the water in her matter; happiness and carefree spirit played a great part in my barging life, none of us had any scholarship. Dear father had hardly known the difference between a smoothing iron and a gridiron, and mother was only about half a class wiser. But the girls, my sisters, did have a little more schooling, but Bill and myself taught ourselves what we knew. The girls were older than us, but it wasn't long before me and Bill could tell them a thing or two. Yes, not knowing any different, me and Bill thought the wide world wasn't a bad school to be at, as well as a good playground.

And so I wondered whether there ever was anything else in the world worth having. I just doubt it; it's a handsome life for those that were born and were schooled into it, for those who studied it and took pride in it. The skill we had were a great asset to our noble calling. Every lifetime passes like a flash out of a gun, so much so that the things that count to make life worthwhile vanish before you know it, and leave you resting on one's oars. But I have to thank God for what I have got. My Rosie, the dear lady that had her bustle badly disarranged at the Tivoli Music Hall seven years ago, my wonderful wife.

Rose and George Winn portraight photographs when in their thirties.

Time marches on, and time can change everything. Wouldn't it be an asset to the human race if that green-eyed snake, jealousy, that couldn't be nice, couldn't be nasty either - do you follow me? God speed, and so we floundered about the dear old

Thames for another four years in this bundle of tricks called the *Elizabeth*. The Museum would have been a more appropriate place for her. I don't think I ever done a voyage up and down the

---

[4] Clout: A piece of cloth; in this context, the barge's sails.

Thames without someone passing some insulting remarks about
the old *Elizabeth*. In fact, she was never a place for a parson, the
fancy words I shouted in her defence, when someone was telling
me to give her a handful of grass and someone else asking me
which end was which.

I've have often wondered if any of these old sailormen
kept a record of some of the answers I returned. Before one was
finished some other expert would always step in and want to
know if we wasn't afraid she would tip up. One of the skippers
had his wife on board. Once I see her standing in the cabin
scuttle hatch, but when he asked one of these questions, I see her
pop down the cabin to save her embarrassment when I told him
in some choice words why she didn't tip up. I met him and his
wife in the street some time afterwards, but this guy didn't want
to know then whether the old lady had tipped up, or whether she
was afloat or sunk, apparently enough was as good as a feast, but
how these shouts across the water used to pass the time. One had
no sooner had breakfast, that's if you was lucky enough to get
any, and gather one's wits for the warpath, and it was dinnertime.
So much so that in many cases the hours passed like minutes,
always sure of a salute of some sort from any passing craft.
Someone called "When the old lady has pups skipper, give us
one, will you."

As you have heard, she was swimmy headed and she
always used to cock her stern up. She was peculiar on her
waterline but surprisingly handy. She was the talk of the Thames,
but I earned a lot of money with her, the work was arranged for me
so I could, but never in the history of sail was there ever such an
ancient novelty.

In passing, although this profession is, or was, a twenty-
four hours a day job, I still think it's the happiest and healthiest
environment one could achieve. Walking the carpet and getting
away without getting the sack, now and again, had added much
glory to this life-long programme, but some wasn't so lucky of
course. Everybody didn't take charge of this old 'Pantomime
Lady' but only the chosen few, and heaven help them that did
during the last ten years of her life. Brother Bill steered clear of
the old bugger; he done the laughing, as did the others, especially
when they'd noticed I had stuffed her cracks up with the mud. But
Elizabeth was the master of all this, you'd no sooner bunged one
hole up and she would make water some where else, and it was
beyond me to find out where all her cracks were, try as one did.
But I well knew she had some, believe me, but it's good not to
know what she had in store for us.

In all my years in this profession, since starting with Bill,
my brother, when I was eight years old, holidays were not in the
programme, but that was about to change.

CHAPTER VI CYCLE RIDE

On July 25th in the year of 1898 I went on a cycle tour from my home at Sittingbourne to Lands End in the West of England. My first place to visit along the South Coast was Brighton on Sea. I had a lovely half-day there and spent the night. It was a most delightful place to spend a few hours, and it was quite a change from work. Being the first week's holiday I'd ever had in my life, it come to me more enjoyable, perhaps, than it did to most regular seaside holidaymakers.

George really enjoyed his stop at Brighton, which was then the most fashionable resort on the south coast.

I arose the next morning and partook of a nice ham and egg breakfast with tea, and then left Brighton for another day's run, my distance so far just 68 miles. On the day of the 26th, I wended my way through all the seaport places of Worthing, Arundel, Chichester, Havant, Southsea, Fareham and a few more places unmentioned, and on for a sharp spin into Southampton where I stayed at a friend's for a short time. I then proceeded on my journey to Christchurch where I ended my days run and retired for the night. My distance was 111 miles in 8½ hours, including stopping for refreshments. I then partook of a light diet and I was quite ready for it. I had a walk to keep myself in circulation and then to bed.

Up and about at 6.30 a.m., I had a brisk walk, then breakfast, and then on the wheels again. I left Christchurch, slipping on through into Bournemouth and had a short stay there of about 15 minutes, making off again in my westerly direction leaving Poole to my left, then crossing country into Wareham. It was country roads and forests, which were very rough and hilly and most chronic for my well-being, to be sure. After a while I was nearing the coast at Bridport, and there I alighted for some refreshment before I proceeded through Devonshire.

Devonshire is a county that is not an enticing place in parts for cycling. It was about time to cease riding again for the night, as the day was getting well spent, nearly 8 o'clock. I had never ridden in my life before on such roads. My run that day was only 90 miles in 10½ hours. I was also ready for my tea again, which was had at the Temperance Hotel in Honiton. It was rather a late one, but it was better late then never with me at that junction. I then retired to bed, which was not an up to date one. Perhaps they thought I wasn't an up to date customer! At any rate I slept alright.

I arose next morning, the 28th, and commenced in the same direction. I was rather an early starter that day, so I didn't have any breakfast until later on. I went creeping along, whistling and singing, and it was a splendid July morning. I passed through Exeter and other places and had ridden about 45 or 50 miles when I stopped for egg and tea breakfast, bread and butter with it of course, and then journeyed on west.

Everything was going on in the best order until I'd just entered Cornwall and the rain came down. Things wasn't looking very lively with me soon after that. But I still stomped the old bike round, but I was neither whistling nor singing, and I think the harder I pushed the pedals the harder it rained. It poured for 3½ hours. In spite of the bad weather I kept on moving and did 38 miles in it and got a soaking. You can be quite sure, readers, that I was wet through, as my attire was very thin and scanty - knickers, sweater, flannels and a very thin jacket was the total of my clothing. But the rain stopped after I had got nicely soaked and the sun came out and I began to dry up like sparrows after rain.

I had further to go before I finished my days 'pleasure' - dear me, what did I say, pleasure was not really the word for it. But before I finished the day's run I was nearly dry again and soon arrived at Truro, my resting place for the night. That made my distance 111 miles that day, and my course had taken me through Exeter, Okehampton, Launceston, Camelford, Wadebridge and St. Columb and other villages along the way, and my time was 10½ hours. I stuck to my light diet as follows - tapioca and custard, with

George's route took him over the ancient bridge at Wadebridge, Cornwall, built by the Reverend Lovibond in 1460 to link the parishes of St. Breock and Egloshayle across the River Camel.

George photographed astride his bicycle at Gibson & Sons' Mounts Bay Studio at Penzance.

tea and other dainties, and then took a short walk, and the wooden hill[1] was my last journey for the night. I was only 36 miles from Land's End.

My last few miles westward were on the 29th July and after a short spin I stopped for breakfast at Redruth; ham and eggs with tea. Then it was on to Penzance, arriving at 9.25 a.m., where I enjoyed myself for half a dozen hours, before heading to the Land's End. There I had a quiet hour and a half and indulged in looking across the Atlantic, or the Western Ocean, with my spy glass, before returning to Penzance where I put up for the night. Dear reader, I had then ended my westerly adventure which amounted to 404 miles in $35\frac{1}{2}$ hours riding.

[1] Wooden hill: Informal synonym for stairs.

I was up next morning sharp at 5.30 a.m., 30th July, to commence my easterly journey home from Penzance. After feeling a good benefit from my night's rest, I then bathed, but it was only my face and hands - in fact it was the only part I had time to wash on this tour, even hardly that some days. At any rate, I'm all ready for a start and was on the wheels at 6 o'clock smart; preferring to work up an appetite before breakfast. I pushed off for 40 miles and then took breakfast, which was brown bread and butter with tea. Allowing myself 30 minutes to eat it, I was then back on the road. My route was to Plymouth, and a splendid road it was too. After an hour or so I found myself at Taw Point, near to Plymouth, making my time 6 hours and 45 minutes, the distance covered 90 miles. Crossing the river by ferry, I was soon in Plymouth Town, where I had dinner, and afterwards took a short look round which amounted to three hours.

Another town, another photographer, George and cycle pose for the camera of Coupe & Bennett Photographers, at 16 Bedford Street, Plymouth.

I set sail again "I beg your pardon, policeman, is this the London Road?" "Straight on." he pointed. I thanked him and travelled on, but not at a very fast rate in the sunshine. Just before reaching my resting place for the night, my progress was interrupted. Probably owing to the day being very hot and the many miles I had cycled, my chain had stretched unnoticed and departed from the back cog wheel, resulting in a snapped spoke.

I spent a few moments securing it and soon arrived at Newton Abbot where I finished the days run, the time 7.40 p.m., the distance almost 140 miles, riding for 10 hours and 10 minutes. I then went into a temperance hotel and had tea and cold ham with pickles. I asked the waitress "Madam, have you got a bed to let?" "Yes, sir." she replied. "I will have it, thank you. As I am anxious to start early," I asked. " about what time could I leave in the morning?" "We don't open on Sunday, sir." She said. "I realise that, but couldn't I leave here at 5 a.m.?" "We don't open on any Sundays, sir." I declined to the hiring of the bed.

So I had a walk down the street and knocked where directed. "Beg pardon; could you put me up for the night?" "Yes, sir, bring your bicycle in." And I wasn't there many minutes before I was quite at home. I then performed my usual habit, washed my face and hands, then a stretch of the legs before a supper of bread and cheese, pickles, and coffee was the desert. A little later it was time to rest for the night. After a good sleep I arose at 6.30 a.m., had the usual bath and a blow before breakfast, then returned for ham and eggs and passed the usual compliments to my hosts.

On the jigger[2] again at 9.15 a.m. leaving Newton Abbot for another days run. But the day was so very hot I couldn't do any great distance, and if my memory serves, most of my journey was on long country roads through more villages than towns, though Exeter and Wells were on my route. It was one of them sort of days when a man don't care whether he works or plays. As I rode, the heat was difficult to bear, but I came across farmhouse, and stopped to ask if there's any milk and eggs to be had for refreshment. Knock, knock. "Have you any milk and eggs?" "No, sir. We've got milk and lemonade." "That will do nicely, thank you." So I got as much of that down as I thought I could do, with homemade bread with cheese, and then pushed off again - and the sun was hot, without a doubt. It was nearly 9 o'clock before I was put up again for the night and, to tell you the truth, I wasn't sorry. Despite several stops for refreshments that day, and long ones most of them, up to an hour, it had still been hard work. But as I have told you, hard work never did harm.

I was in a small village six miles from Bath and the distance from whence I came that morning was 111 miles. "Do you take supper, sir?" asked the lady of the house. "Yes, ma'am. Thank you." Cold mutton and mint sauce she served, with lemonade and milk. But it was no feather bed this time to lie on. I had to perch in the parlour, but it was all right for I didn't make troubles of trifles - and I'll just tell you what the bed was. I had two choices, one was a small size bed and the other was a large size bed, so I couldn't grumble at that - but one was the armchair and the other the floor! Not being a particular chap I chose the floor and I'll be bothered if I didn't sleep a treat. My Sunday had not been a day of rest, and to tell you the honest truth, I didn't ride that day for pleasure, I rode because I was homeward bound and wanted to be there on Monday, by noon, but the remains of my journey when I started out was 275 miles or thereabouts, and I had not succeeded.

I arose next morning 5.30 a.m., 1st August, had a trim up and then off for a longer spin today than any I've done. My cyclometer tells me 155 miles to do. Very well, I'll have a try. So without any more lost time I was at it, pushing off for about 35 miles before breakfast which I took at Calne; ham and eggs, with tea. After leaving the breakfast table, I was back on the road doing a fairly good pace. I overtook the town of Marlborough in Wiltshire and then ascended a very challenging hill. Just as I had reached the top, my back wheel buckled and disabled my bicycle. Unfortunately I had to return to Marlborough for repairs, which detained me for

---

[2] Jigger: Any kind of mechanical contrivance, in this case George's bicycle.

about 90 minutes; very fortunate indeed I was to get the repair done straight away.

I then had to ascend the hill again - not a very good way to cover the ground, to have to climb the same hill twice. I made the top again and then it was downhill doing a fairly good pace, not exaggerating when I say 18 miles an hour. I should think not more than 4 miles from that hill I nearly collided with a pleasure brake, owing to a little girl running from behind the vehicle, so near that I felt the wind pass between my hand and the wheel. You can guess what the result would have been had I struck.

I cycled on past Camberley and other places that I can't describe to you as I didn't note them down, and it is somewhat difficult to keep it all in one's head. After a sprint along the Bath road I stopped to have some refreshment. 45 miles in two hours and 45 minutes - and then I'm at it again. Presently someone shouted "Hi. You're scorching along." But I think it was the sun scorching me. I was going so fast I couldn't easily stop as I had a fixed wheel and no brake. So my extra on the level made up for some of the miles lost on the Devonshire and Cornwall hills I had to climb.

Rose Cottage was a welcome sight for George after his longest day in the saddle. Rose Cottage, 35 Goodnestone Road, Sittingbourne, was the only detached house amongst long terraces all provided by Smeed Dean for their workers. In total, the firm owned 340 houses in the district.

I stopped for tea in Leatherhead and decided to head north, passing through Hampton Court, Brentford and Kew, Kensington, over Westminster Bridge and through south London to the Old Kent Road. As the day wore on I passed through New Eltham and the scene became more open. I was at Rainham, Kent, before the light faded and I dismounted to light my cycle lamp[3]. I had almost ended my last day's run, soon reaching my destination, Rose Cottage, 35 Goodnestone Road, Sittingbourne. My distance that day was 155 miles in 15 hours, the time riding $12\frac{1}{2}$ hours. I had travelled a total of 850 miles, riding for 69 hours and 40 minutes to Land's End and back. It had taken 8 days and I did not have a single puncture. Next day I was back to work.

---

[3] Whilst George's cycle had no brakes (other than a fixed wheel sprocket) or gears, it did have an acetylene lamp. This comprised a container of water which dripped onto calcium carbide powder, producing acetylene gas, which was burnt behind a glass lens.

CHAPTER VII   THE OLD *ELIZABETH*

The *Elizabeth*[1] went from bad to worse. One day she refused duty and wouldn't swim, so she sunk trying to get into Sheerness. A government tug came to our assistance and picked me and the Mate up and took us ashore, offering us any other help we required as soon as we landed. Many thanks to the Government's Navy, they are grand lads. So I sent a wire home, short and sweet, 'Come to Sheerness, *Elizabeth* sunk.' Mr. George Andrews, the Manager, come himself instantly, arriving all hot and bothered and gazing at the wreck with his 'titter - tatter' muttering and eyes like saucers. "How did it happen?" said he. "I think her bottom's fell out." I replied. "Her bottom fell out?" he repeated. "That's about it, I should think." "Dear me, George," Mr. Andrews continued, calling me by my first name, no less, "she's a handful, isn't she?" "She's wicked enough." says I "You never knew when she was going to burst, but I knew she would. I know her, Mr. George and I'm convinced that most of her trouble is in her bottom."

Eventually she was raised and we got her home to the firm's shipyard where she was to be repaired and overhauled. There was a board meeting with the directors concerning the affair. I gave a full description of her problems and one of our directors, Mr. John Andrews, our Manager's father, was addressing me about her. As I suggested before, he was a blunt, rough, uneducated, kind of a man and a man we all fought shy of when we could.

"You seem to have a full knowledge of her bottom, mate." Mate was his usual address to all us men, Captains, Mates and boys alike. "Yes, sir," I said, "I have. I've wintered her and summered her and slept with her, and I know all her tricks." "Yes, mate, we're convinced you do. We are also convinced you done your utmost to save her, getting her in shallow water before she turned over. While she's on the yard she will be in your care, to have done to her anything you and she requires."

"Well, to be candid, sir, the whole of her bottom wants screw bolting up so that it can't wriggle when she's hard pressed. I have mentioned this to the Foreman a time or two, and he said he's examined her bottom each time he's blocked[2] her." "This time, mate, she's in your hands and take this note to that effect to the Foreman. That's all, mate." So I arranged all this work and thoroughly done her

---

[1] *Elizabeth* of Faversham, built Aylesford, 1812, 49 tons. - See APPENDIX A.
[2] Blocked: Placing the barge, or any flat-bottomed vessel, over timber baulks, or 'blocks', spaced to support the hull when the tide ebbs, enabling access to inspect or work on the vessel's bottom.

bottom. Naturally, the Foreman was annoyed, but it had to be swallowed. He was a Londoner and thought he knew better. I know some of these gentlemen don't take kindly if they can't do what they like to some of these old barges. The fat's in the fire, but it was me that had to work her, so I looked out to have her bottom as I wanted it.

But when one's wore out, one's wore out, you can't get away from that. You strengthen some of their old limbs and you think, 'Bob's yer Uncle' for a year or so, but take advantage of 'em and push 'em a bit harder and it upsets their other weak spots. So much so that when they get to that age one has to be careful what one's doing and it's always on your mind. It's a grand life and always something to think about!

The *Elizabeth* was at the shipyard and put on the blocks. There are two of these blocks built with baulk timber to set the barges on, so to get at their bottom for repairs. But the *Elizabeth*, being a weak and old lady, needed four to hold her shattered ribs and bottom on. But my protests wasn't taken into account and never was what she suffered. So the work was in progress and I'm walking about the yard keeping me eye on the old bugger and I thought her head had dropped a little. I nipped on board and lowered the rigging about half way down to put weight on her forestay. But you wasn't allowed to touch the rigging while the barge was on the blocks. Down come the Manager, Mr. George Andrews, all hot and foaming at the mouth. "What're you doing, Captain? You know you're not allowed to do this on the blocks." Exceedingly angry with me, he was. It was a crime to do this, on account of the straining caused to the craft.

As he rushed here and there I kept as close to him as I possibly could, and that wanted a bit of doing. I was waiting for an opportunity to approach him to explain why this had to be done. At last I managed to get his attention. "Pardon me, sir, will you allow me to explain - her head's falling off sir. I've lowered the gear in this position to hold it on." Dead silence. "Look sir, look for yourself." He looked, and then he looked at me and he grinned and silently walked away from the *Elizabeth*, the clown of our fleet, and what a Circus.

So one evening in the early stages of our repairs, our clever London Foreman was digging about round the old girl's stern and made a hole in her side just below the water line. He forgot to block the hole up before he went home in the evening, leaving the old girl's hold as dry as an empty barrel. During the night, up come the tide and run in this hole. Mr. George, our Manager, had already given the Foreman orders to put another block under the old lady's head to stop that from falling off, which he wouldn't take from me, but no one knew anything about this hole, only the Foreman. I think he had got it in for me because he had got to take orders from me, I was the 'doctor' and was responsible for the medicine I arranged for the old barge.

So down we all went the next morning at 6 a.m. sharp, an hour or so after the labourers who were there to scrub the hard down and clean it for the men to work under the old lady's bottom. One of the labourers come to me first, and he stuttered as soon as he see me, nearly choking his self trying to tell me what had happened. He said "Ge - Ge - George, yo - yo - your bar - bar - barge's bot - bot - bottom has fe - fe - fell out." I said "Blimey, what the blazes…" and I jumped aboard and had a look round. The Foreman's already creeping round the *Elizabeth* but don't say a word to me. Half the bottom 'as fell out, and everybody as silent as the grave. Mr. George, the Manager, is there at ten past six the same morning, walked on board the old lady, looked down the hold, had a word with the Foreman, and away he went. Mr. George Andrews never gave me a look or spoke.

But I'm holding the 'trump cards'. I had noticed that there was a water stain right round the *Elizabeth* inside, two feet six inches high and as straight as a line. The barge was as dry as an orange box the night previous when we all went home and I'm wondering how the water got in. So I approached the leading shipwright, a pal of mine - we were in this same firm as boys. His name was Bob Dunham. I said to him, "Nice kettle o' fish here, Bob." I said, and had a little chuckle. "There ain't much to laugh about." Said Bob. "No, but it's no bloody good crying, is it? I asked if he knew how the water got in. "Don't you know?" he replied. I said that I had no idea and he told me that "The Foreman made a hole in the side yesterday and forgot to block it up. I've blocked it up this morning, but don't say I told you."

Do you know what he has told the Gov'nor? Said Bob "No, I do not." I replied. "Well, he said that the cause of her bottom dropping out was through you sinking her at Sheerness, so the Gov'nor has told the Directors what had happened to the barge, and the cause of it - through sinking at Sheerness."

So at eleven o'clock the same morning, down came the Directors, Mr. Hambrook Dean, our firm's Chairman and Mr. John Andrews, our Gov'nor's father, to speak with the Foreman. One of the Directors said to him "Serious matter, Foreman." "Yes, sir." He replied. "Due to the sinking at Sheerness, I understand?" "Yes, sir." repeated the Foreman, with a look as if he'd been given a bottle of rum. But my turn's coming and his 'bottle of rum' smile should disappear a bit quick.

So I had another smoke and up to the Office I went. I saw the Head Clerk and asked if I could speak to Mr. George Andrews, the Gov'nor. He came from the inner office out to see me and seemed very angry. I said "Bad job about the old barge, sir."

Mr. George Hambrook Dean J.P., Smeed Dean & Co. Ltd. Chairman.

Mr. John Andrews, one time Foreman, went on to become a Director.

"It is, Captain." He replied fiercely. "I understand you've learnt it is owing to the sinking at Sheerness, sir." "I gather it is." He replied, with a bit of spit on his lip. I'm dying to keep him there as long as I can, then I'm going to tell him something he didn't see for himself, although he was a shrewd man.

"You know that the *Elizabeth* wasn't making any water when we got her home from Sheerness, because you was on board most of the time, sir. So how did the water get in the old barge on the blocks, all high and dry?" The Gov'nor's still hot and bothered and getting more so. "Water." he roared. "Yes, water." I said. "The Foreman has told the Directors, your father and Mr. Dean, that it was through the old barge sinking that caused her bottom to drop out while she's on the blocks with nothing in her. How did forty tons of water get in the barge on the blocks? That's what I want to know."

Mr. George is flabbergasted, and I'm in good trim. "What's all this about water inside her?" he asked. "Did the Foreman tell your father, sir, that he had made a hole in the *Elizabeth's* side, below the water line and forgot to block it

The barge yard and the large shed where the company's barges were first built, sometimes rebuilt, and maintained.

up before he went home last night - did he tell the Directors that? Because if he didn't I'll see that he does." The Gov'nor slewed round in his chair, his manner quite normal, then he rose from his chair and I continued. "The tide come up and got above the hole that the Foreman had made and the water rushed in. In it come until the tide ebbed below the hole and finally left the barge altogether, when the weight of the water inside took her old weak bottom away from her floor timbers. Did the dirty dog tell the Directors that, the dirty rat." Mr. George, the Manager, our Gov'nor, looked at me very concerned. "Go down aboard your barge." he said. I did, and he was there very near as soon as I was.

He had called the Foreman and was looking down into the hold. There was the dumb witness, a straight line right round the inside of the barge. The Gov'nor called me and asked what the wet mark was. I told him it was where the water had been, two feet six inches in height. The Gov'nor turned to the Foreman and ask him if he knew how the water got in the barge, and he said he didn't. "Let's go and have a look round her." said the Gov'nor, and they come to the place that had been blocked up that morning. Mr. George asked the Foreman if he knew anything about the place they found and, caught out, he admitted he did. "Alright," said the Manager, "you come to the Office tomorrow morning, 11 o'clock."

Next morning Mr. John Andrews set about him thick and heavy, not altogether for what he done to the old barge, but for putting the blame on me. After his tirade at the Foreman, he was given a months notice to quit. It was my turn at the Office next morning at 11 o'clock. I went before the Directors. "Well, mate," says Mr. John, "all I have to say to you is that we have nothing against your good name here, so carry on as you wish to get the old barge repaired. That's all, mate." "Very good, sir." I volunteered and was out of the Office like a shot.

There was no such thing as getting reinstated in our firm in those circumstances and what else could I do, it was him or me, and I'd done nothing wrong. As you have heard, I'm a lifesaver, not a life destroyer, and a receiver of this Country's honours for that. Of course, this Foreman was nothing to me, he was only getting what he deserved.

And so the old *Elizabeth's* bottom was jacked up. I might say, these old girls have got into a pretty bad state by the time they have to have their bottoms jacked up. It's one thing to put tar and hair poultices and a bit of putty in their cracks, yes, but by the time it comes to the 'jack', well I ask you, they're in a pretty poor way. Even all that refastening and new timber doesn't stop them making water.

There was always something about these old things' bottoms, especially at her age, between 80-90 years old. Mind you, she'd done her bit over the years without having anything done, but that was our people all over, as long as these old-timers could drift about and work without sinking, they didn't waste any time or money on them.

Well, after the storm, the shipwrights go on with the job to repair the old barge, with my instructions what to do with fishplates, screw bolts and nuts. They were used, by the hundred, to screw her old bottom up to her aging floor timbers. Never in my barge career did I see such specimen, and when it was done, her old bottom was stronger than it had been for many years. Although, even after all that work, to have filled her with tar and set her alight would have been the better remedy.

But we didn't have that choice, but hoped that this was the last scene of the last act for her. But there was no such luck, it's the old story about cats having nine lives, but this old cow had ninety. But we had been having fun with her and that give us the courage to endure her. And it wasn't her end by a long chalk, she was a damn long time dying.

So the jacks and mallets and mauls[2] were ringing out like a peel of bells at a wedding and everybody seemed just as happy, except the Foreman, and in about five weeks the old lady was in the water again. There she was with a brand new bottom and her holes bunged up with tar and hair and coal tar putty, her rigging with her red sails all spick and span, like a carnival queen, and Mr. George, our Manager, all smiles.

You talk about our beloved King and Queen at the launch of one of our dreadnoughts; just a mere birthday party compared with

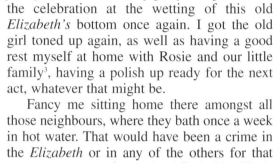

the celebration at the wetting of this old *Elizabeth's* bottom once again. I got the old girl toned up again, as well as having a good rest myself at home with Rosie and our little family[3], having a polish up ready for the next act, whatever that might be.

Fancy me sitting home there amongst all those neighbours, where they bath once a week in hot water. That would have been a crime in the *Elizabeth* or in any of the others for that matter - a waste of soap (and flesh like lilies). Naturally, Bill had popped along now and again to give us a look and talk matters over during our refit, with a laugh and a joke of what Father would say if he could pop along and see us now - "You and I both skippers and roast beef on the table - and father thought we should get indigestion if we asked for more than two slices of bread and butter, and told us we should have to 'draw our horns in', as if we'd been having kippered salmon for tea. Do you remember

George's brother Bill, born 27th May 1866 at 4 Danvers Buildings, Chelsea, was brought up in the family sailing barge tradition.

Bill, when you used to kid me to ask dad for another slice of bread and butter so as he would let go at me instead of you. They were tough times, boy, but we didn't know it. If Dad could pop along, Bill, you and I with a gold ring on our fingers..." "Yes, but what would our Dad say?" asked Bill, to which there was, of course, no answer.

So the next day one of the brickfield foreman gave me my orders where to go to load flint. This was because flint or ballast was the only suitable cargo to carry under the circumstances, for when these old girls have been out of the water for a while they dry out and open their cracks. Put afloat again, they take in a good quantity of water before they close up and have to be watched for the next few days.

[2] Maul: A hammer, in this case probably a pin-maul with pointed head one side for driving bolts and spikes.
[3] Rose Winn, following the loss of their first child in 1891, had given birth to their second, George Charles Winn, on 21st February 1897.

Knowing these things are part of our profession and, if you'll allow me to say, we considered ourselves second to none at nurturing these old dames. If the red sail bargemen with fifty and sixty years experience of these old girls don't know what they want, well, I don't think it's much good going abroad to find out! Red sails in the sunset, on the Thames, what a sight it was. And what a noble life, London lightermen, and red sail bargemen, the cream of the land. But how short our lives often are; just a span of the hand, from thumb to small finger, then to the unknown. Of course that doesn't happen to everybody, but to the happy-go-lucky chap life's just a song. I, with other people in this troubled world, have had some nasty knocks in the nut, I'm sure you'll pardon me, but I never knew what trouble meant, laugh when your heart says so, it will never rise again by sleeping.

We're afloat again and brother Bill is still passing up and down the Creek with his 'Cheerio' and a wave of the hand to me until we meet again in the Thames or some wharf in London, dear old London. The Foreman shipwright's gone and never did say goodbye to me!

And so we're off again with a brand new cabin and the good wishes of Mr. George Andrews, our Manager, to some wharf in London with a cargo we couldn't damage. But don't run away with the idea that because the old *Elizabeth* has been screwed up and her holes and cracks filled up with this, that and the other, to stop her making water, that you could set her about anywhere you liked without watching her. No, that would be the last consideration. A new cabin, mind you, instead of setting her alight on Guy Fawkes' Night. It was, after all, November 1898 when we finished trimming the old bugger up. If ever there was a man who learned the bad language of his country on account of his barge, it was then and it was me, I hope you'll pardon it, so much so that I nearly forgot the national language.

For the next eighteen months or so I blowed to and fro in the Thames with the wheel in one hand and the pump in the other, as the saying goes, and you can well imagine what the Mate had to do as well. As I have told you, if you couldn't do two or three things at once in this profession, you might as well have been in

Smeed Dean quarried local flint for road surfacing. It was an ideal cargo for a barge which was likely to leak, having just come off the yard after repairs, until her hull timbers 'took up'.

After the *Elizabeth's* hull had 'taken up' she returned from flint to brick carrying. Loading bricks was a labour intensive task, the bricks brought aboard in barrows and passed into the barge's hold for stowing.

Madame Tussauds looking at the Wax Works, because you would only have been wasting your time. But what a grand life for those who could.

And so with the wear and tear the old *Elizabeth* got weaker and weaker. Nearing the end of 1900, Mr. George come to me and said "What can we do to the old barge while we build you a new one?" That was a nice surprise. "Nothing at all, sir, because she'll soon sink with the weight of bolts, spikes, and iron plating what's holding her together. I've improved her bottom considerably but it's tearing her other parts adrift close to her bottom, and that's where she makes her water. The tar and hair has worked out of her cracks, sir." He looked at me and said "All right, George," and half grinning, "look after yourself. I leave it to you, the new barge will be built in less than six months." and went about his business.

My twenty-four hour days went on as usual. I had wondered many times what people went to sleep for; it was quite out of the question with some of us. I am sorry to say our lives were too short to waste time sleeping.

To and fro we went, while the mauls and caulking mallets rang out on the new barge like the bells of St. Martin's in the East. She was designed by me and our new Foreman, Bob Dunham, who was promoted to the job when the previous Foreman got the sack. The time was near at hand to say goodbye to the *Elizabeth*. One more voyage to London and back to Sittingbourne. But that wasn't the last of the Old Bugger, and a few other names I called her besides, but they are not suitable for printing here. But it's the beginning of the last 'act' so far as I was concerned, and I am still one of the actors, and Rosie's[4] in the know as well and was never out of it, and what a pal, the girl that didn't lose her bustle at the Tivoli Music Hall, the Strand, London, in December 1889.

After many more trips up and down we arrived back at Sittingbourne with the dear old lady *Elizabeth* and went on the yard with her for the last time. The new barge was built and finished, bar the shouting. It was June 1900 and everybody was getting hot and bothered because she's going to be launched in a couple of days or so. The Manager was flying about like a kite with no tail. "George." he shouted to me, "Yes, sir." I answered. He beckoned me to join him by the old *Elizabeth*. There's this old girl, 88 years of age mind you, water running in and out of her old bottom like a spring running out of a rock. "Take everything out of her that's any good; we're going to sell her." "Sell her?" I said, "Sir, I should never have thought you could have given her away!" "Nonsense," he said, "we want £300 for her. Don't you think she'll fetch that? She's going 'under the hammer' you know."

"Yes sir," I replied. She's been going under the hammer ever since I've had her - and the pitch mop. If the would-be buyers knew as much about her as I do, I should have thought about £3 with some good pumping gear thrown in." I think that jarred the Gov'nor a bit. "Look at her, sir." He half grinned, but we took the good stuff out of the Old Bugger and put in anything that would blow her to London!

The Foreman asked me to take off the stem blocks, the ones that were used to heave up the rigging and lower it down. The rigging was down and I tried to get the bolt free from the block that was attached to the head of the barge, but I couldn't move it. I called the Foreman. He examined it and sent one of the boys to the forge to get a big sledgehammer, called a 'Monday' hammer and it weighed 28 lbs. Now this old bundle of tricks called *Elizabeth* had a square head, swim headed she was. I'm about 27 years of age and I'm sure you'll allow me to say, I could swing this twenty-eight pound hammer as well as the next man in the Yard. If they only had the presence of mind to stand clear - of course, I wasn't a full-blown shipwright journeyman.

I was standing on the starboard side forward, and the Foreman, the port side forward. Now, this will kill you - it nearly did him - we're standing about level with each other and you can imagine after pumping this old barge about for four years my muscles was similar in power to the 'Monday' hammer. The Foreman said "Give it a blow, George. The pin of the block." I did, and unfortunately I hit the pin, but not a true square blow. The hammer flew up and hit the Foreman in the face, knocked him

---

[4] Before George left the *Elizabeth*, Rose had given birth to their third son, Harold, on 27th January 1900.

flying and senseless, badly disfiguring him by the loss of two teeth. The weight of that hammer took me to the deck also, but I was only bruised. Some of the men saw this, of course, and were quickly on the spot. We soon got him to come around and then cleaned him up a bit and got him home. The Doctor was called to give him a survey, and he was passed 'Not serious.' I might say in passing, that I was not carrying a full head of steam m'self. I've got a bruise on the left side as black as the Ace of Spades and about the size of a saucer.

The Gov'nor was in London that day on business; Mr. George Andrews, the Manager, I mean, but we always addressed him as the Gov'nor. Bob, the Foreman, crept down to the shipyard next morning feeling a bit stale, half his face in sticking plaster and looking a bit seedy. I wasn't exactly running either. Bob was a little nervous of the Gov'nor. Down he came at ten past six and you could almost set your clock by him.

Me and Bob's on board this old floating pond called *Elizabeth*, all shaped up as if we're going to do something. Everybody's as quiet as mice, Bob looks as if he's been in the Battle of Waterloo; standing where it happened, explaining to the Gov'nor what had occurred. I'm aft busy doing nothing, and doing less after he was gone. I could see the Gov'nor looking aft at me every now and again, and presently he came to me. "Are you hurt?", he asked. "Just bruised a bit, sir." "Just bruised a bit." he repeated, and looked at me as if I was a fool.

He gave Bob orders to go home for as long as necessary, "… and you," He said to me, "do you want to go home for a few days?" "No, I don't think so sir. I got a bruise plaster on. I'm just a bit stiff, that's all, sir." "Very well then, I leave it with you." and away he went. So me and Bob had a chat. "What did the Gov'nor say?" "He blames it on to me," says Bob, "for not getting one of my own skilled men to do it." It was a near thing for poor old Bob, and home he went, as did I after dinner, to have a breather until the next morning. Bob was back within a week and the work went on as usual, with a knowing grin now and again, pleased that we were alive. They were some of my happiest days.

After a while we had got the old girl fitted out with all odds and ends and leftovers, and out of the Creek she sailed. What a sight she looked; these old things are light headed as well as having a head like a lighter. She was cocking her starn up like a Chinese Junk and just as unsightly. She was on her way to be sold under the hammer in London, and to my relief it was the end of the leaky and tired old *Elizabeth*, at least as far as I was concerned[5].

[5] The *Elizabeth* was sold by Smeed Dean, and continued, despite her weaknesses, for some years in trade. She is recorded sold for further service to R. Salmon in 1910. - See APPENDIX A

CHAPTER VIII   THE ENGLISH CHANNEL

The new barge, named the *Esther*[1], was launched with great celebration, the Foreman and shipwrights as proud of her as I was. In the space of a few weeks she was all fitted out with masts and sails and all requirements from an egg-cup to a flying jib, finished and ready to go. She was a picture, like a new yacht below, and on deck, and quite superior to our coveted 100 tonners, for she will carry 135 tons.

Bill, my brother, stood on board her admiring, and exchanging mariner's jokes. I thought that if father could slip along and see us, Bill and me, as Captains of these barges, and our good wives and families, he would turn tearful with joy. For that moment our two minds were quite empty of anything else in the world, and the whole of our careers flashed by us in an instant. I think Bill was a little bit jealous of my new barge, but I shared with him as much as I could of the moment.

You can imagine my feelings towards this noble looking craft, after four years with the Thames running in that old *Elizabeth* and me and the Mate pumping it out again. It sounds a bit hollow to dwell on that, doesn't it, but everything had its advantages - if you'll allow me to tell you in passing - I was well developed on account of that old bugger, with a chest like half a barrel, with all me other natural parts to match. With a full head of steam, I was ready for anything at our game, as well as another new barge for the dear old Thames in our barging lifetime.

You talk about millionaires; they never new what life was; at any rate, not as I understood it. The ups and downs made it so, and those millionaires will probably never know what they have missed. The humming of the wind in the gear; the thunder and lightning, and the rain beating in one's face at the wheel. Putting about from the port tack to the starboard tack and the sails flacking like successive claps of thunder, until she fills off on the new tack. Always a double portion of rain to encounter while she's in stays or going through the wind, driving rain and rainwater shaking of the sails.

The Mate forward, tending the foresail bowline, suffers the same deluge as myself. The storm abates and the rain and weather in general moderate, and for me and the Mate it's off with our oilskins and we're in another world, but still with taut sheets and as much wind as we can do with. Then the lights of dear old London

[1] *Esther* of Rochester, built Murston, 1900, 50 tons. - See APPENDIX A.

Esther took George out of the Thames for the first time. Dover was one of the busy ports he visited, with the English Channel a challenge awaiting.

come into view, flickering similar to the White City or a Gala Night at the Theatre, and I swear by the hook block[2] I don't know where else you could equal the fun. I'm certain the millionaire doesn't get it.

You finish your tide's sail, it's high water and you anchor at Erith or some other place in the Thames. It may be two in the morning or some other time, and we have a meal and, in passing let me tell you, we're quite ready for it, and as you've noticed, my lifetime just one continual holiday!

So with this lovely new barge called the *Esther* I went further afield, as far as Lowestoft, Yarmouth, Margate, Ramsgate, Dover and Folkestone, with the English Channel staring me in the face as if to defy me to venture further, with fortune staring at me and Rosie. The whole four and a half years I skippered this noble little barge, I was enjoying life to the full, and our Rose Cottage in the bargain too; I was the millionaire of my world, pure and simple, full of the joys of spring, whether winter or summer, without the worries of the Stock Exchange ringing in my ears. You can imagine my Rosie upstreet, as it was called in our locality, with her bassinet pram and our baby Esther[3] in it, with her bustle to match, and me

Sittingbourne High Street, where George and Rosie enjoyed their new-found status and prosperity.

---

[2] Hook block: The large double sheave mainsheet block which hooks to the traveller which, as its name implies, is free to slide across the width of the barge on a timber known as the mainhorse, controlling the sheet of the mainsail.

[3] George and Rosie's fourth child was born 9th March 1902 and named after the barge.

coasting. Our noble Mr. & Mrs. Winston Churchill would have looked rather small on the same side of the street as us, me with me bowler and patent leather boots, and we hardly knew whether we were walking up or down the street. They were the days!

And so the time arrived for me to leave this noble little craft known by Rosie and me as the Floating Bank, the *Esther* I mean, and there was nobody more sorry than I was. As you have mentioned, our firm, Smeed Dean & Co., had a large fleet of sailing barges and one was called the *Persevere*[4]. One day I arrived home with a cargo of coke for our cement works and the *Persevere* was lying at wharf, idle. She was a noted barge in our firm, bigger than the *Esther*, but she'd seen sixteen years under her keel by then. She had done well in the short coasting work and had taken many thousands of tons of material to build up Clacton and Frinton-on-Sea, as also had I.

One of my pals come to me all hot and bothered saying "There's a freight of cement to go to the Isle of Wight and the skipper of the *Persevere* wouldn't take it, and the Gov'nor's annoyed and telling people he's got orders for goods and no one to take the cargo." I slipped up to the Office for my freightage and the Gov'nor paid me. I'm all hot as well, but not bothered like my pal. "I understand you've got a cargo of cement to go to the Isle of Wight, sir, and nobody to take it?" "Oh," said the Gov'nor, "who said so?" "You can hear the bargemen talking about it on the wharves. Put it in the *Esther*; I'll get it to the Isle of Wight, or wreck her trying!" I was just warmed up, you know! The Gov'nor half smiled. "You've never been to the Isle of Wight." said the Gov'nor, "Neither had I been to Lowestoft until you sent me, sir." "I can't take the risk, George." He replied, still with a grin on his

George's life-saving prowess continued throughout his career afloat. He was the proud recipient of this Royal Humane Society Testimonial on Vellum which records the rescue of six boys at Shotley in 1905.

---

[4] *Persevere* of Rochester, built Murston, 1889, 58 tons. - See APPENDIX A.

face. "That's alright sir, only don't go running around telling people you've got a cargo to go to the Isle of Wight and no one to take it." There was not another word from him, or me, and I went about my business, but I heard him laugh out loud when I got outside the Office.

The Gov'nor sent for me the next morning, and after the usual polite exchange of greetings he said, "If I decide not to give that cargo away to an outsider, will you take it to Cowes?" "I'll take it to New York, if no one else will." The Directors in the Office chuckled. "Very well," said the Manager, "we consider you as our leading man, and you must shift over into the *Persevere*." "Just for the one voyage, sir?" "No, permanently, to do the Isle of Wight work." He said. "I don't want the *Persevere*, sir. I'm satisfied with the *Esther*, sir." "Yes I know you are," answered the Manager, "but she's better in a sea than *Esther* and much more suitable for the Channel; but I'll give you till 12 o'clock tomorrow to decide, but we look to you."

The *Persevere* was George's command for nearly a decade. Her bowsprit unshipped, seen deep laden, she works the estuarial trades in later life.

What would you do chums, do it and chance your luck, or not do it and chance your luck - that was the exact size of it, if you see what I mean. I've got to do it haven't I. There was no choice but to stand by them, sink or swim. Being annoyed at this was no good, but a Treasure Trove was in the offing, between the Devil and the Deep Sea. As it were, the other bargemen were yarning and arguing about me - "Now he'll drown his self." "Not him." said another, "He'll never bloody well be drown." "No, I know he won't." said George Simmons, "He's too bloody cunning to be drown." and so it went on. You know, don't you, that I'm very sore about this, but not disheartened, because the *Persevere* was a famous barge in barge life, but there were no privileges in ploughing up the English Channel.

I have mentioned in my remarks what I had inherited before this time. If there's two horses pulling a cart along, the horse that does most of the pulling gets the hay, and that's what it amounts to when it's all summed up.

So I did my very first cargo of cement to Cowes, Isle of Wight, and back to Sittingbourne, and had a 'Well done.' remark from the firm. And for eight more years and a half I ploughed up the English Channel, with brother Bill as Mate, visiting two-thirds of all the ports from Sittingbourne to Penzance, in Mount's Bay, with grain from London. And I did our own work, private work I mean, with many tough nuts there were to crack in that time. The barge *Persevere's* name rings in many of those south and west of England ports, especially Plymouth, Southampton, Cowes, Par and Dungeness as a roadstead, and Poole and Portland. And how many times I found myself 'dead beat' in the struggle to reach these places through rough weather. What I would have given for the chance to have laid down to sleep for a few hours; but it wasn't to be thought of, despite being washed like a half-tide rock, with some of our sails in ribbons, and enough salt round one's eyes to last on the table for a week. But it's all in the days work, and they were some of the extras that came my way for telling the Gov'nor not to go running round the wharves telling people he had got a cargo of cement to go to the Isle of Wight and nobody to take it.

One of two dozen letters to George Winn from George Andrews from the period when *Persevere* was in the Channel trades. Bad weather and damage is a persistent feature of the correspondence.

Towards the end of those eight and a half years[5] the *Persevere* began to work her bottom about and make water now and again, and me and the Manager begun to talk to each other

---

[4] During George's time in the *Persevere*, Rose gave birth to their fifth and last child, Norman, on 19th August 1907. A letter from George Andrews to George Winn at home in 1906 expresses 'sincere sympathy' for a bereavement and refers to Rose's 'weak condition' and offers George any help they may need. As there are no recorded bereavements in the family at that time, it seems likely that Rose had given birth to a stillborn child in April of that year.

like two Shipbrokers do. When these barges do begin to weaken it's usually round their bottom. He agreed with me that it was so, and while we were debating this I told him I wasn't happy with things the way they were. My comments tightened him up a bit, but the Gov'nor wasn't a man to be dominated by anyone, and I got the feeling that this moment was the beginning of the end for me with Smeed Dean & Co. He had offered to build me another new barge of 180 tons and for me to design her to my own plans for the English Channel trading, but our friendship was coming to an end. In other words, it seemed to me, if you want to fall out with anyone, do them a favour and you soon can. That's the exact size of this, and for the rest of my service in this firm it was wit against wit, so to speak.

I was confronted with some awkward approaches from the Gov'nor and it was clear things were unlikely to get any better; so I sent to him my resignation. I heard he was apparently not only dumbfounded, but a bit puzzled as well. I took my things home, sat down and had a chat with my wife, Rosie. Then, down I went to the barge, got the ship's papers and handed them to the Gov'nor at the Office, but he wouldn't take them from me, so I left them on the desk. A few sharp words was passed by me and him and I left the Office for what I thought was the last time. The Directors were more or less annoyed at this and couldn't understand it as they knew about the planned building of the new barge for me, but they didn't know what had gone on between me and the Manager. They wouldn't let it rest. "What's he left for, George?" the Director asked his son, the Manager.

This third letter in four days, following that shown on page 95, was sent to George, indicating that he had taken the *Persevere* down Channel when other skippers would not make the trip. A transcript of all the letters appears in Appendix C.

I knew from experience Mr. George Andrews' father, the Old Man, we called him, was as hard as nails. He used to carry a stick and we used to watch that when we had him to deal with, and

Loading cement in sacks at Smeed Dean's Murston wharf. A leaking barge and a cement cargo were not happy bedfellows!

if there was any arguments between Mr. George and any of the Captains and the Old Man come along, he would go up to them and say to the Captain, "What's the matter, mate?" If he didn't like what he heard it was "Sack him, George." We didn't used to enjoy ourselves when the Old Man was about. He'd tell Mr. George to sack one Captain, and he would look at another, and look out if you started whistling. When the Manager was on a few days holiday, and we had the Old Man to deal with, quite half of our skippers didn't need to take Epsom salts, so scared they were.

"I can't understand this, George." He said, referring to my resignation. "He's left, and no proper explanation. You must get that man back, George." All this I learned from pals who had overheard it. The news became common knowledge, but I didn't want to go back, I knew where I could go and get a living and I had something just under £1,500 to my credit, and I'm sure you'll pardon me when I say I got it by hard slogging and a loving, careful wife!

Within a week the Gov'nor sent for me to go and see him at his house. I went out of courtesy of course. I was shown into his room where there were only me and him - I could see he was all worked up. "Well, George," he begun, "you've done a foolish thing," "Yes, sir," said I, "and not the first one either." The room fell silent for half a minute. "We've just had a telegram from the Captain of the *S.D.*[5] He has collided with the Forth Bridge, in Scotland. He's got her ashore but she's full of water and he is to be discharged when he arrives in London. Will you take charge of the *S.D.* when she arrives back?"

---

[5] *S.D.* of London, built Murston, 1902, 99 tons. - See APPENDIX A.

The *S.D.* was a big sea-going barge. She would easily hold up to 300 tons, but carried 260 tons to sea, and was skippered by outside men that had been on the coast all their lives. She had several Captains over the years. Called the *S.D.*, the initials of the firm, she was heavily ketch rigged. None of us London bargemen wanted this barge, of course. She was flat-bottomed and, for whatever reason, was very awkward in running before a strong wind. Although she was a fine barge, as barges go, from my understanding of flat-bottomed barges, no rig in the world suits them like the spritsail rig. They were born sprit-rigged and in my opinion no other rig would ever suit them, even if their sails were made of silk or satin!

"I'll take charge of her on the grounds that you allow me to take the ketch gear out of her and put sprit gear in." "I don't think our people will agree to that." replied Mr. George Andrews. I thought to myself, they will before I have anything to do with her. "Thanks for your consideration, sir, but she's no good to me as she is." "I could probably settle it," said the Gov'nor, "but I shall not. You come down to the Office Monday morning and see Mr. Dean."

John Hambrook Dean was a son of the Chairman of the Company. "You've heard the news about the *S.D.*?" "Yes, sir." I answered. "Will you skipper the *S.D.* if we give you a free hand to rig her as you want her, and work her in the usual way by finding your own freights on the coast?" "Yes, sir. I will." "Very well then, that's settled. And if you want to come and work in the shipyard until the *S.D.* is ready for you and be paid Captain's money, you can." "Thank you very much, sir. I'd rather have the break if it won't make any difference to you." "As you please." Mr. Dean concluded.

So the *S.D.* was patched and raised and towed up to Grangemouth where she was bound. A number of weeks passed and in the meantime, as I had become a tidy size noise in the firm, I done my utmost to get the late skipper reinstated, but that turned out to be beyond my scope. He was a good man at his job but he didn't know the kind of 'diet' flat-bottomed barges required.

I'd often wondered what a Gentleman's life was, or what it felt like, and with time on my hands I had the chance to find out. Well, let me tell you, it isn't worth a ha'penny candle with a damaged wick. I used to stroll down to the shipyard when I wanted to, and take a note of a few figures so I could work out what I wanted made for the new rig when the barge returned, and as I strutted about I suffered a few insults - What had I done with my millionaire's high hat and was I standing for the next election? Well, as far as the election was concerned, I had already won it, not a parliamentary one, but being offered one of the biggest and best of our firm's fleet.

The high hat was quite in order for me in the old days gone by, with my back against the tiller, and a vamp[6] on the concertina. What glorious times my young skipper days were. Can you wonder at the years flying past like days. I'm still confused as to whether life is what one makes it, or whether some phenomena makes it for you, neither does it matter to me. I recall I made some quick dumplings once and mixed them with self-rising flour in a mistake, and when I went to have a look to see if they were running round in the pot, they were running up the cabin stove chimney instead, with the pot lid on top of them, as black as the stove. There was no time to make more, so they had to be trimmed up for dinner. The only difference it made was that nobody wanted any treacle pudding for second helping, but the sea gulls didn't shake their heads at it!

Oh yes, and the high hat; well you could, now and again, find one in the refuse when loading at Lambeth Vestry, all clean and ready for wearing into the bargain. They were a lovely finished article and these hard-headed City business men was a real feature bobbing about on the Corn Market with their silk high hats, more or less on the back of their heads, buying and selling. I was waiting on my shipbroker, day after day, to see if someone had bought five hundred quarters of wheat or barley or oats for me to take to any port in the English Channel. More

The London Corn Market, often referred to as the Corn Exchange, Mark Lane, was where merchants rented one of the 64 boxes, or stands, where their business was done and the ships and barges chartered to move the grain.

---

[6] Vamp: To improvise an accompaniment; to create a tune or melody.

often than not it was at a very low rate. I've had to do it once or twice for ten pence a quarter when cargoes were scarce.

There's no doubt that some of these business gentlemen were in the same boat. I'd often wondered why I hadn't got their brains, not that I altogether wanted them, but just wondered why, but I never envied them theirs. I always had my barge to go back to, which I could ponder over and play cards, when the time came, with my crew, and have enjoyable evenings, so why would I want to be a silk hat millionaire?

After a while my leisure weeks promenading began to feel as if they didn't fit me too well. I went to the Office to see the Gov'nor to ascertain the movements of the *S.D.* and found the barge was detained at Grangemouth. I had a short chat with the Manager about the different rig that we hoped would be an improvement. I said that I now preferred work in the shipyard until the time arrived for me to join her, which he agreed, although I could see he didn't want to kiss me exactly.

I joined the boys in the yard for my £2 a week, and the old routine passed the time like being at the Music Hall, and some three months went by altogether. Whilst I was on the yard I was sent for, to go to the Office and discovered I'd slipped up a bit. "I see you're at the yard at 6 o'clock each morning, Captain." said the Manager, our Gov'nor. "Yes, sir." "Well it's not necessary for you to do that; make eight, that will suit us." "Thanks very much, sir." "And I'm inclined to think," he went on, "that you'll be a barge owner, one day." He looked at me with his piercing eyes, for which he was noted. I laughed; that tickled me a bit - that had never entered my head. "That's all then." He said in dismissal.

I returned to the yard where all the jokes were, and that twenty-eight pound 'Monday' hammer I knew, and so did Bob the Foreman! I don't think I ever handled that hammer again, by the way.

The Office had me in again where the Gov'nor told me that the *S.D.* was ready for me to take over at Lymington, Hampshire, sailed there by another of the outside skippers. So I travelled down to Lymington[7], on the Solent, and took charge of the *S.D.* I got in touch with the brokers, Haddon & Beavis[8], in Southampton, and fixed up four cargoes of stone from Alderney in the Channel Islands. It was the first time I had been to this island - what a place to live. Portland with two cargoes, and two for Southampton and from there, 260 tons of old railway chairs for the West India Dock,

---

[7] George took his eldest son, George Charles Winn, by this time 17 years old, to ship aboard the *S.D.* as Mate with him.

[8] Haddon & Beavis were long established shipbrokers and coal merchants with premises in the High Street. William Beavis is well remembered in the locality for providing a £10,000 gift to Southampton Corporation in celebration of victory in W.W.I to provide the Beavis Treats, an annual distribution of sweets to local schoolchildren.

London. Then it was a cargo of coke home to Sittingbourne and home, discharged at our firm's cement works.

I wasn't long doing these six cargoes, which left me with a nice little balance sheet. But don't think because the wind had blown into the north-west that it had knocked the bottom out of the stormy green weather that had previously raged between me and the Manager, and that the coast was clear for ever. Oh no, he was waiting for the fruit to ripen, and then the harvest would be over. I'm waiting for that time to arrive, sooner or later!

So it was onto the shipyard for the alterations, which took ten weeks altogether. For me it was another holiday at home with Rosie while I'm altering this ketch rig barge *S.D.* to sprit rig, as much as a hobby as for my living. We're getting along with it like a house on fire. We're all helping each other. There was only one difference. Bob, the Foreman, wouldn't allow me to do any striking with a maul or a hammer! We got over that all right and I did something else instead. Bob knew what he was doing, so I left it to him and inside the ten weeks we were all fitted out

George Charles Winn's Certificate of Discharge records that he joined the *S.D.* on 14th March 1914 and left on 2nd. September 1915.

sprit rigged and a grand sight she looked as barges go. She was well approved of by the heads of the firm and the Manager. They hoped the alteration would improve her actions at sea. From my experience of my toys I had no doubt that ketch rigged she was a perfect cuss running before a stiff breeze, and no one man could steer her alone.

She came off the yard and I'm loaded with a full cargo of cement for Southampton and away we go. We had a following wind after we rounded the South Foreland and enough of it to go along comfortable with. To my delight one man could steer her with ease. What took two men to do with hard work before, as well as the *S.D.* wanting six and eight points to run in[9], she would now run before the wind in three points, so help me God if I lie. I was as proud of this achievement as if I'd had to pay

---

[9] The compass is divided into 32 points. When running before the wind craft were inclined to yaw from side to side of their intended course, the yaw measured in compass points. Converted to degrees, the *S.D.* yawed 60° to 90°, but when sprit rigged, just 30°.

for it. The cost of this alteration was something under five hundred pounds sterling.

From all angles she turned out to be a lovely barge to work, and with a cabin as large as an ordinary room of a house, in other words Buckingham Palace to me. So I plunged about the English Channel, including France and the Channel Islands, up to my eyes in fun, as well as water at times, and making good returns for the owners.

One year and some months passed and the 1914-18 War started with Germany. Wise men begun to throw money about and fools were catching it. That was the last thing our firm would stand for, if they could avoid it. I had just discharged a cargo of stone at Shoreham, from Cherbourg. I had a hell of a passage across Channel to Shoreham - I knew we were in for a wet journey when we started, but that was all in with the rest of the fun in these flat-bottomed craft, especially with a beam sea. I lost one jib, one shroud broke and a five-foot sky light smashed. Although she was a mountain of a barge she looked pretty small in this circumstance, but was as strong as a rock, and no pumping to worry about. That's a big asset to one's mind at such times. The distance was about 89 miles, as the crow flies.

The English Channel's a drafty place at times, I can assure you, for small craft in such weather, and fortunately for us it was round about high water when we reached Shoreham Harbour or I should have had to run up Channel to Eastbourne Roads or Dungeness. I was about eleven hours doing this journey and we call that pretty good going in these craft. After mooring at the Shoreham jetty, I found I had got a ten-inch list to Starboard, but I had some idea that the cargo had shifted before I arrived, and was rather glad I hadn't any further to go. I got unloaded and so I'm up and at it for another cargo to some part of the world, with a telegram from my Southampton ship broker Haddon & Beavis offering me a cargo of ammonia for Granville, south of the Channel Islands in the north-west of France in St. Michael's Bay.

It's Saturday, and there's not much business done in this line on Saturdays, so I slipped home to Sittingbourne for the weekend and run down to the Office to have a chat with the Manager about the business in general. He said "If you're not fixed when you go back to Shoreham, come home here and load cement for Torquay and wire me your arrangements." So I sailed home for the cement and arrived there in due time.

At the Works I was told to go in the berth to load. Then the Foreman told me not to. "The Gov'nor," he went on, "said he wanted to put 100 tons into another one of our barges first. Having loaded the 100 tons, I was about to go on the berth when it happened again. 'Ah, ha,' I said to myself, 'we're in for some fun as sure as the Lord made little apples.' They kept on doing this for nearly a week. I saw Mr. Andrews near the berth. 'Right, Gov'nor.'

The Smeed Dean Cement Works where the raw cement was packed into jute sacks for loading into the firm's barges or lorries for more local or inland deliveries.

said I to meself, gathering my courage. "I'll wait on you at ten minutes past six tomorrow morning, sir." As you've understood from my remarks previously, you could set your clock by the Manager's punctuality, and he had schooled some of us into that groove, and a very fine custom it was. It taught me what everyone should know and act on, and never once did I let him down during my stay with him - and thirty-five years isn't just a winter or a summer.

He had his good points and I knew he was Manager; that was quite in order. So down he came all hot and expectant, and slipped into the cement shed. He could see me standing on deck without looking up. I jumped onto the wharf waiting for him to come out, and out he come and I led off the debate. "Haven't you got anything else for me to do other than shove about the Creek for fun, sir? "That's my business." said he. "I should have thought it was mine as well." said I. "If I want you to shift every tide for a week I expect you to do it." raising his voice. "Do you mean to tell me that you don't know, when you give me orders to take the berth, whether you want me in the berth or not?" says I. "Look after your own work." he roared. "Do I look after it?" I shouted in reply, "I live in her night and day, and you say that to me." He looked at me, as a good mother does at her three-month-old baby and said "I'm sorry George, if you don't like it, you know what you can do." "I've known this was coming as long as you have, sir." I'm finished and he had achieved his ends.

CHAPTER IX   OWNERSHIP DISASTERS

There's no such thing as being at one place too long or too short. Life is a lottery - whatever happens to Man is fate and my experience taught me this. A man does not have to have an exceptional brain to become a professional bargeman, but he must have good and long experience and above all a good and sound nerve once he meets trouble at this game; he's a man finished young, otherwise.

So it was home to Rosie to talk matters over for a week, then to London for a look round. In London I was in and out the brokers' offices, among the bargemen and the hustle and bustle of the City gentlemen. "Hello, old man. What are you doing? Where's your ship." That touch me a little bit, but the feeling soon disappeared. "'Ello," said Joe Besant, one of my ship brokers, "Where's the *S.D.*?" "I've left her, Mr. Besant." "Left her?" said he with surprise. "Yes, me and the Gov'nor couldn't quite fit, so I thought this was the best way to get out of it." "Well, the best of luck old man. I must be off. Oh, but just a minute, would you go lightering for Cook for a while if I could get you there?" "Sure I will." I replied, for anything would be better than nothing. "Right," said he, "until something turns up, George. I'll let you know in a couple of hours, boy. I think I can manage it." He pulled out his watch. "In a brace of shakes I must be off. I'm behind, see you presently." He hadn't time to blow his nose, but he had time to help me.

Everybody was behind in those days, even if they were too soon when they got to where they wanted to go! Businessmen rushing about Mark Lane wiping their foreheads, tittering to each other on the market, off the market, the place lined with people, and it's doubtful if they saw anyone else, such was the programme of November 1915. If any of them fell down, they didn't know it without they had to have the ambulance, then I don't think they could believe it, and me, marking time with a gold watch and chain across me chest and a meat pudding and two veg at lunch hour.

Bill, my brother, wasn't in this swim; he was scooting about the Thames in the firm I'd just left, but no doubt thinking about me. But I wasn't doing too bad; I was engaged by Messrs. Cook, lighter owners, as a lighterman for them and after a few weeks I was sent for to take charge of the 200 ton coasting barge *Leonard Piper*[1] owned by Mr. James Piper. And so to the coast again, to blow up the English Channel from side to side - and end to end. I joined her about the end of November, plenty of trade then and plenty of

---

[1] *Leonard Piper* of London, built East Greenwich, 1910, 99 tons. - See APPENDIX A.

money for freightage, but the war restrictions in the English Channel and the North Sea was a hard weapon to have to deal with.

They had but little or no mercy on us coasting craft - not allowed to enter any harbour after sunset, winter or summer alike. You'll have to go there and do this and that, whether you could get there or whether you couldn't, knowing full well you were British and had obtained all the necessary details they required, but no, you must put to sea. The French was no different, and mines that had broken adrift didn't add anything to the fun, but it was your job so you had to grin and face up to it, of course. In the main they were nerve-wracking times.

Years back, as you will have read, we had moved to a big house, a detached, at 35 Goodnestone Road[2], Sittingbourne but by now, me and Rosie decided we should move away from our part of Kent, too close to my old masters and a bit of an industrial backwater. So we ups sticks and finds a comfortable little home, sweet home, at 15 Ramuz Drive, Westcliff-on-sea, a fashionable resort in Essex where, as it turned out, we were to live out our days.

Now these 200 ton barges wasn't easy toys to get, which caused a lot of jealousy, and it was only picked men that was engaged to skipper them, if you'll pardon me. Some of the bargemen were up in arms about this, and it was the main talk among them. One said "Have you heard the latest. Winn has got the *Leonard Piper*." "No?" said another. "He has." said Walter Roberts. "Well, strike a cat stiff." said Jack Beard, "I hope Jimmy Piper (as James Piper was known) loses his high hat." Those barge boys can't get over the shock. They're marching up and down Mark Lane with their hands in their trouser pockets in twos and threes, and their silver watch chain jumping up in the air like a skipping rope, tittering to each other and swearing like troopers, as was their way.

George and Rosie's new Westcliff home at 15 Ramuz Drive.

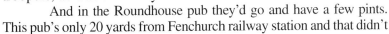

And in the Roundhouse pub they'd go and have a few pints. This pub's only 20 yards from Fenchurch railway station and that didn't

[2] The houses occupied by the Winn family, including George's brother, during their time in Sittingbourne were all in the same locality of Shortlands Road, Goodnestone Road, and Shakespeare Road, and all constructed of Smeed Dean yellow stock bricks, by the company for their workforce. All still exist.

improve matters, because when they come out the air was blue with their own foul-mouth language. Of course, I wasn't with them; they looked out to make sure of that. Back to Mark Lane they would go, freshened up a bit, ready for anything in our ring, and then it was to the Dining Hall, Great Tower Street, for meat pudding and two veg, followed with plums and syrup; that would straighten them up a bit.

One or two of these boys met Jimmy Piper. They were ready for him after having a few in the Roundhouse. They would go on the Corn Market as was usual to do. Jimmy was bound to be on the Market, and a few more similar to him, otherwise the Market was more like a cemetery. Jack Beard spotted Jimmy Piper - "There he is, Roberts, after him." so Walter Roberts went up to him. "Good afternoon, sir." with a bit of sea air attached to him. "A bit quiet on the Market today, sir?" "Yes," said Jimmy, "it is quiet, Roberts." Walter Roberts is wiping his forehead with his red and white pocket-handkerchief. "Ain't much doing anywhere, is things, sir?" "No, Roberts, things ain't too brisk." and Jimmy Piper could speak the bargemen's language quite as fluent as they could, when he had to, as well as knowing something about the art of self-defence, and wasn't backward in showing how it was done if he was hard pressed!

"Well," said Jimmy, "I must be getting along. Did you want to see me about anything particular." "Yes, sir." said Roberts, "Is Winn going to stop in the *Leonard Piper*, sir?" "Yes, I hope so." was the reply. "But damn it all, sir, I've been on the coast all these years and on your back doorstep the whole of the time, and Winn's just got the sack out of his barge." "It makes no difference to me, Roberts, if you had been on my front doorstep all the time, I've engaged Winn as Master of the *Leonard Piper*. You've got a good barge, Roberts, and Winn hadn't. Settle your differences with Winn." But Roberts knew a lot of tricks better than that, and easier one's to, but we were most of us pretty good pals other than a bit of jealousy.

They was 'Dirty Dogs', but it's all in life's programme, but all bargemen don't strike the same note, neither does the millionaire. Who is the millionaire? The man with a million of money, or the happy, happy-go-lucky bargeman that never knew the meaning of trouble - I wonder. No, I didn't join the crude bargemen if I could avoid it, my wife and my barge were my sweethearts, as George Chirgwin said about his fiddle, and that was the keynote of my life. There weren't many murders among us committed! One or two, now and again, was killed fighting, but that was very seldom among the red sail bargemen.

Harold Winn, George's third son, pictured at the tiller of the *Leonard Piper's* lugsail rigged barge boat as he and the third hand set out for the barge anchored off. Harold was Mate with his father, other than when his elder brother George Charles took on the role.

One of the boys stopped a little too long one night with the pub and the girls, then rushed down to his barge to go away. But his barge had just left the Quay. It was a fine, calm, night, but the Captain wouldn't send the boat for him, so he jumped overboard, or rather jumped in the creek to swim to his barge and finished up half way and was drowned. There wasn't much of this sort of thing among such a large crowd of us. But boys will be boys, and from experience some of us know something about this. We didn't mind walking the carpet in front of the skipper; it was the last quarter of an hour with the girl that mattered to us. But if it happened twice, it was the sack for certain.

So for the rest of the 1914-18 War I pushed the English Channel to pieces in the *Leonard Piper*, from end to end and from side to side and many times during this period she shook the wax out of me, if you'll allow me. I was at Saint-Valery-Sur-Somme, France, with my last war cargo of coal, when the good news was brought to me by one of our soldier officers that an armistice was signed, November 11th 1918. We celebrated until November 12th. It was some kind of relief for

The *Leonard Piper* at St.-Valery-Sur-Somme on Armistice Day, all the vessels at the quay bedecked in flags flown to celebrate the end of the war. The *Leonard Piper* flies a long pennant bearing her name from the topmast, presumably last worn at her launching some eight years earlier.

everybody. I think it was about the first time I'd had a basin full of Champagne, some there was prostrate, and it was a bit foggy with me as well. I hardly knew whether I was looking north or south, but if I'd drunk all that was put before me, I'm not so sure I'd have been alive to worry about it. The Champagne was flowing like a spring tide in the Thames.

After about twenty-four hours we begun to slow down and get back on normal grounds. During the jollification one of our fellows who was sitting in the room with us, probably about to get up or not, pitched from one side of the café head first at the other side and knocked himself senseless. We got him to the quayside, which was close by, and lowered him down on the deck with ropes, where he lay for about eight hours before he knew it! But all that mattered for the time being was that the War was ended. During these war years it was tough going in those red sail flat-bottomed barges, both in the English Channel and in the North Sea likewise.

For about the last two years in the *Leonard Piper* I traded to Antwerp, Belgium up the

George Charles Winn, had first joined the *Leonard Piper* in late November 1915, after coming out of the *S.D.* a couple of months before. But he left the barge on 12th April 1918 and this Identity and Service Certificate shows that prior to rejoining his father in the *Leonard Piper*, he was skipper of the sailing barge *Wyvenhoe*. He left his father again, to go as Captain of the spritsail barge *Iverna* in March 1920.

Westerschelde and to the different places there, namely Boom, Terhagen and Niel, and a more dangerous river I was never in. From Flushing to Antwerp is about 48 miles and mostly all long sands, and dangerous ones at that, and the most ticklish river to navigate and similar to the treacherous Goodwin Sands if a ship gets on them.

I met many good people in Antwerp and my name rang there as a friend to the Belgian refugees in this Country during their stay in England during the War. And I was considered best friend and second to none by my Antwerp shipbrokers Messrs. Giani & Muller[3], and was always first in their minds for a cargo. I did exceedingly well in their hands and was offered a good job as Water Clerk for them, but my toy, my sweetheart barge, overruled that.

1921 arrived and I began to think a little differently about my waning life and my little fortune that I had made, which was a few thousand pounds sterling. I never was a businessman, but I knew quite a bit about the job that I was doing, if you'll pardon me. I knew where I could buy a 280 tonner, ketch rigged barge, so I left the *Leonard*

---

[3] Giani and Muller, est. 1868, Antwerp's oldest shipbrokers, are still in business today.

Piper and became owner and Master of my own craft in June that year. Called the *Diana*[4], I joined her at Truro, Cornwall, where I bought her for something less than £2000. After a few days aboard her to get straightened up and to get things ship-shape, I had talks with a Cornish schooner skipper about the vessel that I had just bought, as well as chatter about the usual things that one does in a lifetime, with a laugh and a joke, and he wished me luck on my new enterprise.

We sailed down the Fal to Falmouth Harbour and on to Newlyn in Mount's Bay, where I loaded my first cargo. It was granite for Littlehampton, and I'm very delighted with my undertaking, and when I sailed passed the Eddystone Lighthouse on my port beam, with a strong south-sou'-west wind blowing, and the sea breaking aboard now and then, I thought what a picture I had painted without brushes.

I travelled about for a short time with this vessel called *Diana*, to London, Antwerp, Channel Islands and so on, and during this time I put a four and a half horse motor winch on deck to work my anchors and sails, as she was a heavy to work barge. It cost me something less than £200, and that answered the purpose of two extra hands.

But one day, from the very moment that I cast off from Truro, Cornwall, the swine was one whole source of trouble, would not do as she was told, pig headed, peculiar actions, wouldn't be coaxed. She started to act similar to an obstinate horse with the driver holding his head and giving him a few pieces of loaf sugar and patting him, but then he would walk away as if nothing had happened. Never was I confronted with such a task, I never left her,

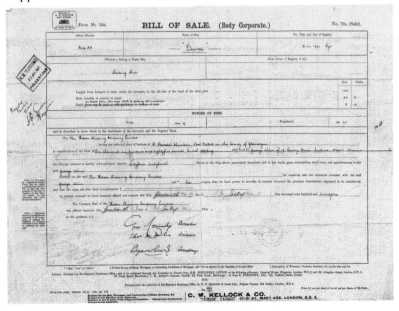

The Bill of Sale for the purchase of the *Diana* on 14th July 1921 for the sum of One thousand six hundred and eighty-five pounds British Sterling. Capt. George Winn's ownership was to last just eight and a half months.

---

[4] *Diana* of Rye, built Rye 1891, 144 tons. - See APPENDIX A.

The *Diana* at sea, seen running before the wind under full sail, including a squaresail, to catch every zephyr on an almost windless day in the Channel.

night or day, but it seemed as if she was waiting for me at every move I made with her.

You know me now, don't you, at this barge game. Well, I'm at one of the Channel Islands; Alderney to be correct, loading my tenth cargo, this one also of granite. My wife, Rosie, is with me for a holiday. I'm well known in this Island and had made many friends there. I was bound to St. Helens on the Isle of Wight. I had only been in Alderney a few hours, quickly loaded and away. The Pilots give me a friendly pull out of the harbour with their motor-boat, and a very fine day it was as one of the Pilots remarked "Here today, skipper, and gone tomorrow." He was quite right, there was but very little wind then. But during the early evening the wind increased from the south and the night looked exceedingly bad, with a light drizzle of rain for some considerable time.

A sudden puff of wind took the square sail to ribbons before we could get it down. I quickly got one reef in the mainsail as the wind began backing against the sun. In a short while I'm close-hauled with one reef in, and standing jib only, mizzen stowed. The wind increased to a full gale. I can't lay my course for the Needles Light, Isle of Wight, so I soldier on through the night, keeping as high to weather as she will. I picked up the Anvil Light on Durlston

The crew of the *Diana*, (L-R) Captain George Winn; the boy 'Cook'; George's son Harold, the Mate; and George's wife Rose. A big ketch with a squaresail would be a lot of heavy work for such a crew; three to five grown men the more usual number for such craft.

Head, south of Swanage at one o'clock next morning. It was April Fool's Day, 1st April 1922. I was hoping to make Bournemouth, or perhaps Christchurch, for shelter, when about a couple of miles east of Swanage the throat halyard shackle broke and the mainsail fell to the deck.

That rendered me to the wide world, helpless. A lee shore and no way out. I fired our distress rockets but there wasn't time for a tug to get to me. The Swanage lifeboat couldn't get to us; for some reason or other she couldn't be launched at that particular time. The *Diana*, with cargo of granite, and four souls aboard, drifted towards the rocks at Swanage. I let go the first and second anchors with sixty fathoms of cable on each, but to no purpose. The *Diana* dragged ashore to leeward and onto the rocks. We took to the rigging, my wife with me, and my son Harold, our Mate, and the cook. Unfortunately, the *Diana* was holed and full of water in less time than it takes to write about it. It was a good thing for us to have got in the rigging. The lifeboat men waited on the shore, with us and for us, until they got us ashore about nine in the morning, with the breeches buoy, as no lifeboat could approach us in those conditions.

At first light, *Diana* is seen ashore in the breakers at Durlston Bay, Swanage. Her sails are being torn from the rigging and spars, and the mizzen mast is on the point of collapse, as the surf batters her stricken hull.

My wife, God bless her, stood up to it manfully and everybody in Swanage was very kind to us, from the Doctor down to the newsboy, and all beyond praise. That 1st of April 1922, what a morning, black as a coal mine and blowing with sleet to complete the programme, and the *Diana* not insured for a brass farthing[5].

---

[5] The *Diana* was insured for the winter months only, her cover expiring on 31st March, the day before her loss.

Later in the day, the waves had broken the *Diana* beyond any chance of redemption. Swanage Coastguard report that 87 years on, pieces of the *Diana's* cargo of granite still appear on the beach after winter storms.

What a smack in the face it was for us all. My wife and my small crew and myself stayed at Swanage for eight days and was well cared for. I watched the *Diana* breaking up rapidly, and I sold the wreck, where she was, to the lifeboat men there.

We returned to our home in Westcliff-on-Sea and I rested on my oars, as the saying goes, with many friendly offers from barge-owners to sail their barges, with a pat on the back. At the time of our

A telegram to others in the Winn family at Westcliff-on-Sea from George Winn, tells of the loss of the *Diana* and that all aboard were saved.

disaster, our lives was my only concern, but not after the *Diana* struck the rocks and I see that my wife could stand the strain; then the world was ours. So here we are, waiting for the next move, and at the same time getting our second-wind for another round, before we throw the towel in, I wonder. I had many good friends that tried to help me, and really did help me, surrounded with warm-hearted people and the heat from God's sun shining on us as it never did at any other time in our lives. With the memories ringing in my mind of that Boxing Night at the Tivoli in December 1889, one of our honeymoon nights when I and my wife begun our lives together; to share what there was, to bear the hand of fate, and never were we blessed with that hand more than on that fateful morning of April 1st 1922 when we were drifting to our doom, powerless to act, but waiting for the end, whatever that end was to be.

Never meet your troubles halfway. You're sure you lose your head in such times and your success will crumble to disaster - cool, calm and collected is the slogan, then fate will do the rest. The last straw is better than nothing, dark and tough the clouds may be, boys, but don't add more weight to them or they will be tougher still. Life is a tough road, especially with wars thrown in, but don't let it get you down, sing as you go and let the world go by, and wait for the dawn - a slogan that will surpass all storms until the blue skies arrive again.

So after a while here we are at the hands of the unknown, all aglow for the next act, and as fit as fiddles for the next reasonable offer of some barge owner. I got a telegram to go to London to see the owner of a 200 ton ketch barge about skippering her for him, which I gladly accepted after, of course, me and my wife and son having a home chat, with a little merriment as well, so as to be braced up with the joys of spring! So we put up a full head of steam and got on with the job, although I would have rather had a 200 ton sprit-rigged barge, but beggars can't be choosers, and I did well with this barge called the *Askoy*[6].

After a year, maybe, I bought her from the owner for a few hundred pounds sterling and slipped around the coast like an aeroplane, with assistance of good friends, especially the Antwerp shipbrokers. With as little sleep as I could manage with, this little craft paid for herself in a brace of shakes, but not without a bit of hard-going, if you'll allow me the phrase. Not all beer and skittles by a long chalk, but it's one's job that has to be conquered, irrespective of the barriers. The sea itself has no respect of customers; you've got to take it whether you want it or not and fate does the rest, and no one can regain what's lost. The North Sea and English Channel is a bigger weapon against these flat-bottomed craft in wintertime, but it's a noble life, especially when one doesn't know anything else!

[6]*Askoy* ex. *Ada Gane* of Harwich, built Harwich 1882, 110 tons. - See APPENDIX A.

The ketch barge *Askoy* was previously the *Ada Gane*, named after the grand-daughter of William Gane who had her built by his friend John Vaux at Harwich. Gane, who owned fishing smacks as well as barges, was to have built the most expensive ketch barge built in Harwich, the *Sunbeam* of 1889. In 1892, when just three years old, she was sunk by the steamship *Ariosto* off Dungeness. The Admiralty Court found that the *Sunbeam* was not showing a stern light and Gane's claim was thrown out. The court outcome and financial loss was too much for Gane who, after the hearing, committed suicide. The *Askoy* went on to become the yacht *Leigh Hall*.

So I'm stepping it out for roughly four years with this little craft called the *Askoy*, not missing a quid for the want of looking for it. And the race of life goes on. So in December 1926 I fixed up with my London brokers to go to Calais, France, and there load a cargo of steel rails for the Tilbury Docks in the Thames. I was navigating up Gravesend Reach on 1st January 1927 with taut sheets - tack and tack - when the unforeseen happened. It was a shock like the sound of a thousand bricks falling through a glasshouse. I had collided with a large steamer that was riding at anchor, or rather my barge did - at my hand of course - unseen, and by then unavoidable. We reckon to be able to put these craft through the eye of a needle and we are noted for our capability of this regard, and widespread at that, pardon me.

The ketch barge *Askoy* under sail in the Thames Estuary.

The *Askoy* is gradually sinking; so assistance was summoned and the tug *Challenge* took us in tow and got us ashore before we sank. She was soon full of water and tide flowing over her. Look at it from its proper angle, the excitement certainly beats cock fighting, I ask you, but the *Askoy*, my barge, was badly damaged.

In 48 hours my barge was patched up and towed into the Tilbury Docks where I was bound and not a wink of sleep for me in that whole time. I made arrangements for my crew's comfort, and my wife and daughter came up to meet me with a motorcar and took me home and to bed. Exhausted, I begun to lose all sense of such a place as bed, but after 24 hours of massage and good attention by my wife and daughter and I begun to think what a mug I looked lying in bed. So it's up again and on with the show, ready for the next act of life's gamble. Medicine is only a sideline compared to a Thames bargeman's life for a cure.

The Elliott Steam Tug Co.'s *Challenge*, built of iron in 1884 was longer and of greater tonnage than the *Askoy*, which she towed ashore.

You'll no doubt note by my simple remarks that if all the land's men knew how easy this profession is they would all be Thames bargemen and there would be no bricklayers or miners. It's a grand life, the fun one gets out of it, when one learns the true meaning of each other's language. Yes, they're a noble crowd, especially when one barge collides with another barge and one skipper don't know quite so much about the profession as the other fellow does, what he

collides with. Then you hear something that they don't tell you in the House of Commons. That is one of the privileges the Thames bargeman has; he does have a free hand. I have known ladies to turn their heads, bargemen's wives as well - that is all in the play where the actors do their stuff. It's a good show chaps, a jolly good show. But during my career I have known some of the actors of this profession to take their own lives by hangin' and drowning at their own hand, as does happen in most big 'schools' in life; life's a lottery and fate is the master.

I have known quite a few topmasts fall down in the topsail spritty barges in not much wind, that being the last thing you'd think could happen. You should have heard one skipper. "Well, strike me dead," said the skipper, "what the ----'s done that? We've only had it six months and there's no wind." "Seven months, skipper." the Mate corrected. "Well, what's the difference," the skipper roared back, letting go at the Mate, "you bloody fool?" With the skipper's anger, most Mates would have to pipe down or he would get a 'fourpenny one'. The Mate's running about the barge with one eye on the Captain and the other one everywhere else within reach, whenever anything unusual happens or, for that matter, at any time when navigation is in progress.

The skipper can't understand this topmast breaking, as only a week, or less, before they were sailing with a stiff breeze and the mast stood to its work. He's still cursing, of course, because there's nothing else for him to do, until he is exhausted for words, and that takes some time. It's a wonderful gift at this profession because it blends so well with what has happened, and you'd be surprised how much relief it is to get it all off your chest. I hardly know myself, what we should do without knowing our two different languages! But the spritty bargemen are a grand crowd, the real essence of humanity, the first to assist a pal when the unforeseen happens. They'll shed their blood when the unfortunate one can do but little or nothing for himself, and wouldn't leave him until the last straw - and yet possibly the day before they'd have punched him in the gob, but that was yesterday.

I well know what I am talking about. Many years ago one of our crowd had a lump of wood with a big nail in it fall on his foot and the nail went through his big toe. There was nowhere to get help. Me and one of the other boys, bargemen of course, operated on him. One had to stand on his foot while the other pulled the nail out of his toe - you should have seen the fuss he kicked up, but he was better in the end for our efforts, and there weren't anybody else around that he could have counted on, if you know my meaning. I could go on for days with the hospital side of my barge life.

Barge: It's a word that's music in my ears, and not only so, but it's food to my body as well, born chewing tarred rope as it were, and what an appetite for my calling. I ended up with a mean few hundreds in capital, and patches on the knees of my trousers, what Rosie my wife put on of course, and a Sunday suit to wear. Some millionaires die at 35 years of age, others get God's blessing of a longer life. If only it was possible for men and women to enjoy life and forget the troubles of the life to which they were born; forget the portion that fell thought the 'sieve' and make the best of what they saved. Why want a college education to build up a career to become a millionaire when one is born a millionaire and the world is yours. School - does the nightingale need go to school? What a tenor he is to sing for us to enjoy. Our lives are too short to waste on education, other than by the school of life.

I may have mentioned that ever life-saving jewel, Harry Williams, the pride of Bromley-by-Bow, London, for his achievements. He was never happier than when he was diving into the Thames, fully clothed, to do something for others that could do but little or nothing for themselves. He saved so many, two pints of ale for Harry, then it didn't matter to him whether he was in the water or out; the cream of humanity. Perhaps he had one suit of clothes, perhaps two, but he lived for you and for me. Think of it, grand isn't it, he was a true millionaire.

The *Askoy* survived the crippling blow of both collision and cost of repairs at the height of the late 1920s slump to be refitted as a yacht. She is seen here in May 1929 dried out off Leigh-on-Sea, by then bearing the name *Leigh Hall*.

So by now I'm fit and ready to return back to the *Askoy* at Tilbury Docks, for the next stride in life. With new energy and a refreshed mind, I discharged my cargo and had the *Askoy* surveyed. The cost for Board of Trade requirements for repairs were between six and seven hundred pounds sterling, but I hadn't that much capital. With much regret, I had to sell the *Askoy* for what she would fetch.

It was a smack in the face, maybe, but it's all in the play. Fate unkind you might say; not a bit of it, definitely no, I am one of the most fortunate men in God's earth bar none, and as fast as a door closed on me, other doors opened.

Within a few weeks I'm among the people in the London of my surroundings, with a smile and a handshake ready to put me back on my feet at the first opportunity; gentlemen with silk top hats at that. Marvellous, isn't it, these busy businessmen. "Have you seen George Winn?" they'd ask some skipper. "Yes, I see him ten minutes ago, sir." "If you see him…" "I'm sure to see him, sir." "...send him round to my office, will you."

I'm there in a couple of wags of a dogs tail. "Hello, old man, glad to see you safe and sound again; how are you?" "Not too bad, sir, thanks." I answered. "Doing anything?" "Not at the moment, sir." "Well now, the *Valonia's*[7] loaded ready for sea and the Captain's left to take a motor ship. She's fixed for a round. She's bound to Newport, Isle of Wight, then to go over to Alderney, Channel Islands, to load granite for Portland and there load stone for London. Will you oblige me, old man?"

It was a return to a sprit rigged barge after George's brief foray into ketch barge ownership. A large and powerful barge, the *Valonia* was well suited to the English Channel trade. This photograph, believed to be of the *Valonia*, sees her entering the West Solent, the Needles astern.

---

[7] *Valonia* of Rochester, built East Greenwich 1911, 90 tons. - See APPENDIX A.

"Sure I will, sir." "Right, that's settled. Get what money you want off the broker, you know the rest, and the best of luck." We shook hands and away he went. That chat took less than five minutes and, before I could get me wind, he was somewhere else in the City.

After I came to and straightened out a bit, I'm half way down the Channel before I got on board the *Valonia*. She was a fine 180 tonner and fast as spritty barges go, and owned by Mr. Horace Shrubsall of Greenwich, and a gentleman as well, in between the strain of life, and he built this barge and others, and fine craft they all were. Yes, those were the days of plenty of the best of everything to eat and no time to eat it.

Ambition and go counter-balanced everything, something to wake up for - that's if one had the time to go to sleep; beautiful isn't it. The spritty barge life without end, the life and soul of the Thames bargemen, paradise without argument, with it's memories of one of the greatest professions under the sun. But don't think I'm alone in this gamble; there were quite a few, as no doubt I have mentioned in my simple remarks before here, but only a small number of us, made it a lifetime Henley Week, and what a regatta it was!

So we're off again, this time with the *Valonia*, with round one of a new contest, but more or less with the same opponent - that tough guy called the English Channel, printed on our forehead, watching out for where he 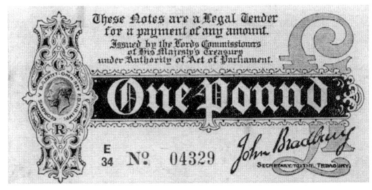 would strike next. My first call was Newport, Isle of Wight, were I arrived in due course, and later completed the round and the three cargoes and was back in London in 28 days. Not even a black eye, and the distance as the crow flies about 540 miles; but one has to do many more miles than that to achieve that distance in these spritty barge craft.

I was very well received on my arrival in London by the owner, cigar and a handshake and a pocket full of Bradburys[8]. Easy, isn't it, money for old rope, why worry about the Stock

Known as Bradburys, these W.W.I issued bank-notes remained legal tender only until 20th June 1920, but the Bradbury nickname for £1 notes appears to have lingered on.

---

[8] Until the outbreak of W.W.I, Bank of England banknotes could be exchanged for gold. To protect England's bullion reserves, the Treasury took over banknote issue with the provision of 10/- and £1 notes bearing the signature of Sir John Bradbury, Secretary to the Treasury.

Exchange? Took Rosie home a bag of shrimps, got on three tram-cars and didn't know it, but I do remember putting the shrimps on the table, but how I got there is still a mystery. I think it must have been Leap Year, or some such explanation, though I didn't believe it because it doesn't make good sense. I have no other explanation, but to somehow get home with out getting stuck on a mud bank was a corker!

I called to Rosie "I've brought you some shrimps." and up the stairs I went like a rocket-bomb, or I expect that's the way I went. After about four hours, I found I was in bed and on the port tack with taut sheets when I woke. I don't think I'd seen Rosie; I was in too much of a hurry to sleep it off anyway. I heard someone shout "George, I'm going out." "Alright love, I'm coming." I answered. There was no reply to that. I had a look around. I didn't feel too good, but I made it down the stairs. I see Rosie looking at me and I'd got my port light on her. I said "Shall we go to the pictures?" To my surprise, she agreed, and I was glad. I didn't feel much like doing a marathon, so the pictures would suit me fine and everything was going splendidly for me, in the circumstances. I had another visit to the W.C. and soon we was on the way to the pictures. I was pleased to sit down, my legs was a little groggy, and we had a nice evening. I said something to Rosie about the picture every now and then; Rosie's look at me but didn't say nothing!

Eventually we got home from the picture house and I begun to feel hungry and said "What have we got for supper, love?" She went to the scullery and brought the bag of shrimps in and said "Where did you get these?" That was a bit of a stinger. 'You do that again,' I thought to meself '- not if I can help it.' I said "I had a cigar with the owner and it certainly knocked me over..." "Knocked you over..." she interrupted, "... a pretty state to get in; I should think you can see that for yourself." She was right, I could, but I couldn't a half a dozen hours before that. But Rosie silently forgive me and we go on with life as usual.

I would have liked the permanent skippership of the noble little barge, the *Valonia* but, naturally the owner had other competent skippers under him, and of course I had to give way. None coveted her more than I did, but the situation had to be endured and command forfeited on fair grounds because sailors, and when I say sailors I don't include the scallywags; sailors don't believe in every man for himself and the devil take the last one, not until the last ditch and the order given by the Captain "Every man for himself." I'm proud to be a Thames bargeman and I don't class myself as a sailor in that sense of the word.

So here I am at home with my wife, at a dead-end as it were, or awaiting the hand of fate, travelling up to London once a week to that grand emporium, the Corn Market, to look for a

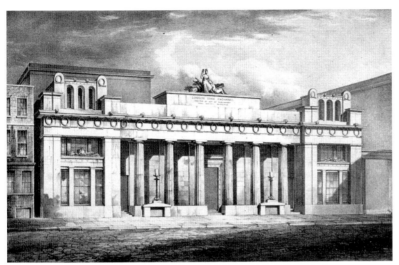

The London Corn Market in Mark Lane was established by Act of Parliament and occupied purpose built premises which reflected its national importance.

berth. I was offered work in a barge yard, but that didn't suit my circumstances. I still had many friends keeping me in mind for the first opportunity, which was a great consolation to me.

Do you know of anyone who have a greater right to their daily bread, if you pardon me being rude for a moment, I wonder? I'm not using my words; this is what the London gentlemen in the silk high hats are saying about me. Penny cigar days rang as loud in my ears as ever and things all aglow, puffing at half a cigar and a pair of Dickie's patent leather boots at 6/11d. a pair. But now I'm wondering why night should ever come; why were we born to such a nightmare when we have only just begun to live, silly isn't it?

Either before or after his passage in the *Valonia*, George Winn took the ketch barge *Ethel Edith* to Calais to collect 160 tons of roofing tiles for Northam in fulfillment of a Charter-party dated 19th April 1928.

Shipped in good order and condition by SOCIETE COMMERCIALE DU CALAISIS *on board the ~~steamship~~ or vessel called the* " ETHEL EDITH " *whereof* Winn *is Master for this present voyage, now lying in this Port and bound for* NORTHAM (Southampton)

a cargo of eighty thousand roofing tiles and one thousand ridges weighing one hundred and sixty tons. ---------160 tons ---------

being maked and· numbered as in the Margin, and are to be delivered, in the like good order and condition at the aforesaid Port of NORTHAM *(below bridge)* (*The act of God, the Queen's Enemies, Fire, Machinery, Boilers, Steam, and all and every other Dangers and accidents of the Seas, Rivers and steam navigation, of whatever nature and kind soever excepted*)

one day and a half occupied for loading

Received twenty pounds sterling on account of freight.

unto order *or* ~~his~~ *assigns* Freight for the said Goods as per charter-party *with primage and Average accustomed.* **In Witness** *whereof, the Master or Agent of the said ship hath affirmed to* **one** *bills of lading all of this Tenor and Date one of which* **one** *bills being accomplished the others to stand void.*

Dated in Calais,April 23rd 1928. Number,weight and quality unknown The Master

CHAPTER X   DEAD MAN'S CLOTHES

Some three or four weeks passed and I begun to get a bit stiff in the joints with no salt water seasoning, and with my machinery more or less at a standstill, waiting for the almighty wheel of fate to stop at my number. Suddenly I have received a telegram to go to London and see the owner of the *Valonia*, and I am gone up there before I could have skinned a cat's tail, wondering as I go whether I was wanted to take charge of the *Valonia* permanently. I get seated in the office with the usual compliment exchanged. "Well, skipper," he began, "I've got some bad news. The skipper of the *Venta*[1] has died coming up the English Channel near the Needles, Isle of Wight, on passage to London. The barge is lying off Ryde. Will you oblige me and go down to Ryde and do the necessary? We are going to bring the deceased home by rail, but we are attending to that, so you'll go down and bring the barge up to Wandsworth; that's where she is bound." "Yes, sir. I will." "Thanks, old man. Here's some money. It's nice to have you about and if you've got nothing in view, even better. It's for you to decide about stopping in her, the *Venta*, I mean." "Thanks very much." "Good day, then," said he, "and the best of luck."

This was a sudden change of fortune and I had to laugh, even if I'd died before I got out of his office, for my stiffness had all gone! But it did seem a strange situation that I had to wait until someone died before I got a job, I thought to my self, although I've been connected with quite a number of these cases of one sort and another. So I slipped home and told Rosie the news, and then down to Ryde, Isle of Wight, the next day, to get on with the job once more. I had a talk with the Police and got everything over and above board, and was sailing up the English Channel the next night.

It was very dark, but a fine offshore wind, with Brighton's lights looming up like a huge fire, but you could hardly see one's hand before you, no craft in sight and every thing more or less as still as the grave, except a drop of water popping aboard to windward every now and again. The cook, known as the third hand, was having a nap in the fo'c'sle. I said to the Mate "You can have a lie down on the locker, too." because an hour in the cabin was worth having if it could be got at any time. He lies down all standing, as we say, in his rubber thigh boots and coat all ready for any emergencies.

I'm at the wheel, which was close to the cabin companionway. Presently, up he come very silently, to have a 'pump-ship' or something. Not a sound of him did I hear until he pushed by me like a flash of lightning. I could hardly see him. Blimey, it shook me for the

[1] *Venta* ex. *Jachin* of London, built Maldon 1893, 70 tons. - See APPENDIX A.

moment, and as he passed me, he shouted "It's dark." and to make it more scary I'd got the late skipper's big coat on what he had just died in, and just for a split second I wondered if it was him stepped back on board!

I didn't say anything to the Mate for the reason of not giving meself away at the time. I've never had any wish to wear dead men's clothes, only I went down to Ryde with a kind of Petticoat Lane fit out, knowing that the late skipper had all sea-going togs for his use on board. I have been shipwrecked a few times, as you have read in the previous pages, but I'm buggered if ever I was jolted as I was on this night in question. So there was nothing else to do but turn the cook out and make some coffee and have a midnight meal to steady things up a bit and renew the energy.

Venta was built at Maldon at the John Howard yard as the *Jachin*, but changed both name and Port of Registry when passing to the Horace Shrubsall fleet.

So here we are ploughing along nicely doing about 6½ knots and well lined up with our meal of a hunk of salt beef; Scotch flank to be correct, and about the size of half a brick! I tightened things up a bit, and tucked our trousers well up[2] so I could see better where we were going. After we had the blowout on the delicious salt beef, I told the boys the story of my little scare a while before.

I didn't want any sleep that night. I'd had about eight hours the night before and that's not too bad for the likes of us. Neither did I go too much on the late skipper's big coat; it didn't seem to warm me like most big coats that I had been used to. Perhaps it didn't fit me like it did

---

[2] '...trousers well up' - A number of reefing points near the foot of the mainsail and foresail have been tied up where the sails hamper forward vision from the wheel.

the late skipper, and that makes all the difference, don't you think; at any rate, I didn't think it did, and that went a long way in my view.

For the rest of the night I felt I was warmer without it, and for the rest of the voyage I could hardly bring myself to look at the damn thing. It was a big Army coat and belonged to one of our soldiers that was in the 1914-18 War in France and, of course, had certainly been over some strange grass in its time. I wasn't used to big Army coats, and there seemed something uncanny about it.

I was never cut out to wear soldier's clothes and had I missed my target, and been called up to join the soldiers' ranks, all I should have required would have been a few extra pairs of clean trousers and would have been warm enough without a big coat. That's if I had lived long enough to have worn the trousers; I think there's some doubt about that. It was also fortunate for me, I think, that the big coat couldn't talk. The Mate and the cook had a good laugh over my little scare, as well as me doing my share of laughing.

Anyway, we're slipping along very nicely and have passed Dungeness the next morning and through the Downs same night and then up the dear old Thames, and eventually arrived at Wandsworth Bridge, Fulham side, and there discharged this cargo of Portland Stone.

You have learned from me that this barge, *Venta*, was on passage from Portland to London when the skipper died; it's an ill wind that doesn't blow in someone's favour and we all experience this at one time or another. It was good to be in harness once more because there's so much fun attached to this game. There's usually someone swearing at you, or you're swearing at them, and usually nothing ferocious behind it. When asleep I have laughed in my dreams, so I have been told, at some of what has taken place when one was in full swing at the job, when awake.

And so all the thirty-two points of the compass are revolving once again at my command, and I have decided to remain in this little hundred and fifty tonner for as long as the hand of fate decides. I telephoned the owner regarding my arrangements and all was to his satisfaction. The deceased skipper's goods and chattels were to be removed by his son when we reached our destination. He gave his good wishes and gifts, including the big Army coat, which made me go cold just looking at it. He didn't know what I was thinking. I knew I'm going to dump it as soon as I can.

I asked the Mate if he'd like to have the coat. He said "No thanks, it's far too big for me." With a grin I said "Yes, so it is for me." I had to think things out a little, so Jim, the third hand, our cook, took charge of it and kept it in the fo'c'sle. It didn't matter what the weather was, no one seemed to want to wear this Army coat. Only occasionally when conditions were really bad, any port in a storm, so to speak, then Jim wore it. Even at that, he kept looking at us, me and the Mate I mean. When it rained I think I got wetter looking at it than I should have done if I had never seen it again, but I had to keep quiet.

CHAPTER XI   A LITTLE YACHTING

And so I am nearing the end of my memories of my spritty barge life, and the facing, as long as fate permitted, of that monstrous piece of water, the English Channel, and of that grand old River Thames, the paradise of all rivers and the playground of the red sail spritty bargeman. I was nearly born on my father's barge, missed by the margin of twelve hours when mother defeated me from being born on the high seas, or on the Thames, as it were, by leaving the barge and taking me with her in a Hansom cab to be delivered to the world at White Hart Court, Chelsea, London, God bless her, on 22nd February 1869.

It was the home where everybody knew her, from Weidner, the pork butcher, and purveyor of Pease pudding and fagots, all hot, on special occasions, of course, for which he was noted, to the pawnbroker with his three brass balls, and that humane figure, Old Mother Lewis, the Queen Mother of our Court. It was Old Mother Lewis passing the news around to the neighbours "It's a boy." in her usual attire, a lace-up boot on one side and a button-up boot on the other side, and frantic with joy and in whose mind's eye I became Prince George of White Hart Court!

The Hansom cab was designed and patented by the York architect Joseph Hansom in 1834. Their low centre of gravity made them quick around the streets of London, in George's case proving suitably fast getting his expectant mother to White Hart Court for his delivery!

The sound of the old Court in my ears renews one's appetite for life - can you beat this paradise? If so, tell me how - or tell the world how. I may be wrong, but I don't think so, and the only thing that I can see that's wrong is that one has to pack up when one thinks it has just begun, and that calls for a bit of digesting. The race of life is more or less run according to history, and nothing can be done about it. Only think, and live with the memories of a happy and glorious life that has flashed past like one summer's night crossing of the English Channel, with not a care in the world. Grand, isn't it, and with a toy that I thought would have lasted me the rest of my life, but fate stepped in and defeated me. Just a song and a laugh, and the show is over.

Well, as I have already said in my simple remarks, I don't know what millionaires call living, but I'd back my life against theirs. As a happy-go-lucky human being, with hardly a dull moment, life is too short to mope and in my opinion not a profession in the world so interesting as life in the Thames spritty sailing barge; just one huge fairground and in the bargain, paid to do it.

I stayed in the *Venta* until 1934, but the time had come to hang up my sea boots. Enough of that old adversary, the English Channel, had soaked through my body. It was time to get dry! Although I had to give up the barges owing to strain, I find it's as hard to be on land, with the routine gone, but what can't be cured must be endured. But, in passing, not sailing in these beloved spritty barges was like parting with one's leg or arm, as you'd say, but I could not carry on with the hard strenuous work night and day after roughly 58 years continually in harness, but I have done a little summer yachting at Southend, close by where we live.

I have acted as Pilot to Mr. G. Lambert's racing cutter *Yankee* of the 'J' Class during this time, and a splendid time I had. A fine Captain and crew they were, twenty-five of them all-told

Yankee anchored off Southend, 5th June 1935, for the racing. Anchored behind her is *Shamrock V*, Sir Thomas Lipton's fifth and last challenger for the America's Cup, by this time purchased by Sir Tom Sopwith as a trial horse for his later *Endeavor* challenges.

including myself. I can't do less than say a little about the *Yankee*. Mr. G. Lambert, an American multi-millionaire, was on board and he sailed her when racing. There was also the designer, besides other friends, and a fine set of people they were. Everybody on board the *Yankee* seemed as one, owner and crewmen alike. The *Yankee's* mast is 153 feet high, twice as tall as a spritty barge's. She is 125 feet long, 22 feet 6 inches in width. Her displacement is 148 tons and she draws 14 feet 6 inches of water.

Yankee visited England in 1935 to celebrate our beloved King George's 25 years on the throne. There was much celebration because it was the first visit of an America's Cup yacht since the *Vigilant* in 1894! The season had started at Harwich, with the *Yankee* to join the racing at Southend. Whilst our racing was full of exciting times, we did not master the King's yacht *Britannia* and came fourth in both races. At least we did not break anything, whilst others in the race lost masts, booms, and tragically a man lost overboard.

The six course meals served for us 25 men was beyond all measure in quantity and quality. My wages was £1 per day, and £1 extra each day we raced. I wish Mr. Lambert God speed and good luck. What a cutter!

Marvellous, isn't it; I sometimes smile at the people who have to work for their daily bread, instead of the play of the red

Lambert's *Yankee* on the wind during the 1935 racing.

sailed spritty bargeman. But it's the same the world over isn't it, someone has to work, don't they? Good exercise for one thing; it keeps one fit and that means a lot in life. Yes, I certainly miss the company of my barges, but I am glad to say I can weather that luxury and the memories are food to me, and grand to fall back on.

When the other chap had a new cork fender aboard his barge and you hadn't, you'd tell him what to do with it. Sometimes he'd get a bit ratty. It largely depended on which it was that told him what to do with it. Some of us had to watch that point, or the other fellow would surely invite you to do it. Yet the cork fender was a coveted toy aboard our barges and you were exceedingly lucky to get one. As you may or may not know, they were used to put between two craft that was about to collide with each other, to take the blow and prevent damaging the barge. You had to keep these cork fenders 'under your pillow' or you'd get them pinched. They were a great improvement on the ordinary piece of grass rope rolled up into a knot, commonly known as a Turk's head fender. If one of the barge boys that was acting as Mate of the barge dropped one of these cork fenders overboard and lost it, he was in for a rough five minutes for certain. The skipper was usually sorry afterwards of course; Thames bargemen wasn't adapted to knocking boys about; but at the same time, they were kept in their place; discipline was their master.

Yes, they were glorious happy years and more to it than I care to remember because I haven't the time. My last few years, as I think you will have understood from my story, have been the hardest during my life's tale, but with some of the happy sailing barge days mixed in, it doesn't go down too badly. My dear old wife

George and Rosie in the twilight of their lives at their Westcliff-on-Sea home.

here, darning my Jerseys and stockings and about the house, is my salvation of these later days, as though we have just begun where we started 60 years ago, with two years courtship included. Just a span of the finger and thumb, and now no more swearing and shaking hands with that noble crowd, the London lightermen. But everybody can't have the good fortune to become a Thames bargeman, however they envy us, no more than I can be a bank clerk.

Speaking of bank clerks, I stepped into a bank at London Bridge with a cheque to collect my freightage, and it was pouring torrents of rain. In the way of a joke, while the bank clerk was eying me up and down - I wanted £60 to be correct - I said to him "I often wished I'd been a Bank Manager." Surprised, he asked, "Why?" a little surprised. I said "Pop outside and have a look." and while he was fiddling about with the cheque and the money it suddenly dawned on him. He give me the £60 and said with a flushed face "Is it raining? I said, "Well, It's either raining or the Thames has gone bottom upwards." and after a slight pause he said to me "I thought you looked wet." I agreed that I was, and slipped off with my freightage.

Let me recall that fateful 1st April, 1922, when I lost my fine barge at Swanage in the English Channel at the almighty hands of fate. What was it, to be compared with the lives of my small crew, my beloved wife and also myself, knocked out as I was with excessive hours about and boisterous weather, and almost powerless to even walk when we were nursed ashore to bed by the grand people of Swanage. No, readers of this, it was not the value of a ha'pennyworth of firewood what I lost.

We are now white about the head, without money, millionaires pure and simple, nevertheless. Grand isn't it; in my opinion there's no other way to describe it. We are white about the head, but what difference does it make whether white or black hair? She, my wife Rosie I mean, still makes a beef pudding when she can get the meat and suet. Fifty-eight years ago I made it when we was on our honeymoon, as I think you know. Well, it don't go down too bad today when you can get one. Oh, yes, I can make them as well and it's something you can set about when it is made; when we save up enough stuff of course.

I sometimes wonder what the rest of the people live for. If I haven't missed anything, what have they got in common - an empty world as far as I know. Yes, the keen and clever things that were done between these sailing barges and steamboats, great and small, passing and repassing each other on the Thames, and only missing each other by feet, and sometimes less when it couldn't be avoided. Many times a 14,000 ton steamer would be involved in this display, missing the sailing barges by a foot; imagine it - by just 12 inches! Then up would go the cap in hand of the Pilot and Captain of these steamers in congratulation of the miracle of these Thames sailing barges missing their ship. This was a common occurrence, and no matter how cold the weather we didn't need a fire to warm us, for swearing at them kept us fairly warm! But I don't think they heard what we said, although we didn't bother about that. Yes, the clever misses, I must repeat, were unequalled by many other craft. But they didn't all miss, by a long chalk. Scores of these Thames sailing barges were put down the cellar, nautically speaking; run into and sunk by these steamers, and dozens of the unfortunate men drowned. But it was a splendid gamble and splendidly played, if you'll allow me the phrase, and not much different to playing skittles at some parts of the Thames below the Bridges.

Our life was a nautical rendezvous, pure and simple, and grand fun for those who had the trump cards and played them at the right time. But don't run away with the idea that a girl in every port was all you needed at this game. The knowledge and experience of my generation and profession is short lived and it is now but a dream, as one who looks back and thirsts for the right answers, I'm bewildered to know. I search back and relive my life to improve on my mistakes. Never mind, it's been a grand day and I have been glad to be with you, but the sun didn't shine half long enough for me - that goes for all good things, but the opportunity and privilege to have them are unpriced - and the Englishman's privilege to grumble guaranteed.

What a grand age I have lived in, perhaps never to return for the common man. For those, I mean, who knew the worth of living and made it worthwhile; for those who made everything a speciality, they are, in my views and practice, the spice of life.

And so then, in my 80th year and to conclude my story, I am left with the happy memories of my child days and onwards. Chelsea and dear old White Hart Court and old Weston the toffee man, and the "Pie hot" man, and the old watercress woman with her cry echoing in the buildings "Jack is Dead" to sell her wares, and a host of others of course. Life is a rough road, but don't make it rougher by dropping your chin - you can face the Devil with truth and win. So cheerio, sailing bargemen, and the best of luck.

George Winn, Sailing Barge Master
Born 22nd February 1869 - Died 31st December 1951

APPENDICES

The reader would be forgiven for assuming that Appendices are the boring bits at the back of a book but, on this occasion, there is much to fascinate and inform in the pages which follow.

Appendix A: More details of the barges mentioned in the text, with thanks to John White, Barry Pearce and Hugh Perks.

Appendix B: Transcript of the letter from the Revd. Robert Payne Smith, Chaplain at Milton Vicarage, dated April 18th 1890, in reply to that from the Archbishop of Canterbury's office of April 17th 1890, regarding the bargemen's strike, courtesy of Lambeth Palace Library.

Appendix C: Transcript of 24 letters from Smeed Dean & Co. Ltd. signed by George Andrews and others, to George Winn, sent between 21st April 1906 and 5th January 1912. From the Winn family collection.

Appendix D: Two postcards sent from France during W.W.I. From the Winn family collection.

Appendix E: Transcript of 17 letters from John Wilks, to George Winn, sent between 14th October 1920 and 6th April 1921. From the Winn family collection.

Appendix F: First two, and only surviving, pages from a log book of the *Askoy* for passage Southend to Antwerp, 25th November to 1st December 1925. From the Winn family collection.

Appendix G: Abbreviated transcripts of Charter-Parties for *Askoy* and *Ethel Edith* raised between 12th December 1925 and 23rd April 1928. From the Winn family collection.

This appendix provides more details of the sailing barges mentioned in the text, captions and footnotes. The sequence of data is barge name first, followed by Port of Registry - **PoR** (next Port of Registry is indicated by a number in parenthesis), Official Number - **ON**, year built - **YB**, where built - **WB**, by whom - **B**, Registered Tonnage - **RT**, owners in sequence from new, though not necessarily a complete record - **O**, eventual fate where known - **F**.

Alabama, **PoR:** Faversham, **ON:** 45558, **YB:** 1863, **WB:** Faversham, **B:** J Goldsmith, **RT:** 43. **O:** J.M.Goldfinch (Faversham).

Alexandra, **PoR:** Faversham, **ON:** 56650, **YB:** 1867, **WB:** Sittingbourne, **B:** R.M.Shrubsall, **RT:** 44, **O:** Sampson Court (Oare); Frederick (Maidstone); Eastwood & Co. (London); J.Trevenor (Maidstone); F.Quilter (Woodbridge).

Alfred, **PoR:** London, **ON:** 24584, **YB:** 1847, **WB:** Bankside, **B:** Not known, **RT:** 33, **O:** Finch Coles; Coles & Shadbolt (Islington), Smeed Dean & Co. (Sittingbourne).

Alma, **PoR:** Faversham, **ON:** 27835, **YB:** 1858, **WB:** Sittingbourne, **B:** George Smeed, **RT:** 36, **O:** George Smeed (Sittingbourne); Smeed Dean & Co. (Sittingbourne); Wm.Steggle (Bethnal Green).

Askoy (Ex. *Ada Gane*, later *Leigh Hall*), **PoR:** Harwich, **ON:** 84033, **YB:** 1882, **WB:** Harwich, **B:** John Vaux, **RT:** 99, **O:** W.Gane (Harwich); Fred Crundell (Dover); George Winn (Westcliff), **F:** Lighter by 1929, converted to yacht, wrecked 1939.

Bessie, **PoR:** Rochester, **ON:** 94559, **YB:** 1888, **WB:** Murston, **B:** Smeed Dean & Co., **RT:** 45, **O:** Smeed Dean & Co. (Sittingbourne); Tom Allsworth (Queenborough), **F:** Lighter by 1941, converted to yacht, hulked Conyer, broken up 1966.

Citizen, **PoR:** London(1), Maldon(2), Rochester(3), **ON:** 9990, **YB:** 1846, **WB:** Lambeth, **B:** Not known, **RT:** 59, **O:** Holloway & Murrell (Maldon); W.C.Murrell (Maldon); Bell & Parry (Queenborough), **F:** Sunk in collision 12/04/1894 at Woolwich, Registry closed.

Diana, **PoR:** Rye, **ON:** 80258, **YB:** 1891, **WB:** Rye, **B:** G.T.Smith, **RT:** 144, **O:** J.S.Vidler & Sons (Rye); Haigh Hall Steam Ship Co. (Cardiff); The Hilda Shipping Co. (Port Talbot); George Winn (Westcliff), **F:** Wrecked 01/04/1922 at Durlston Bay, Swanage, out of Register by 1934.

Edward, **PoR:** Faversham, **ON:** 26258, **YB:** 1841, **WB:** Sittingbourne, **B:** Henry Thompson, **RT:** 36, **O:** Ashendon; George Smeed (Sittingbourne), **F:** Capsized and sank 1878/9, broken up 1880.

Elizabeth, **PoR:** Rochester(1),Faversham(2), **ON:** 26255, **YB:** 1812, **WB:** Aylesford, **B:** Not known, **RT:** 49, **O:** John Huggens; Smeed Dean & Co.; R.Salmon.

Emily, **PoR:** Faversham, **ON:** 10995, **YB:** 1856, **WB:** Sittingbourne, **B:** George Smeed, **RT:** 33, **O:** George Smeed (Sittingbourne); Smeed Dean & Co. (Sittingbourne), **F:** Sunk 1894.

Esther, **PoR:** London, **ON:** 112721, **YB:** 1900, **WB:** Murston, **B:** Smeed Dean & Co., **RT:** 50, **O:** Smeed Dean & Co. (Sittingbourne); T.Shmidt (Sheerness); Sheppey Motor Barge Co., **F:** Abandoned and hulked opposite Stonar Cut 1948.

Ethel Edith, **PoR:** Ipswich(1), Faversham(2), **ON:** 97684, **YB:** 1892, **WB:** Ipswich, **B:** Robert Peck, **RT:** 97, **O:** Robert Peck (Ipswich); William Dines (Sittingbourne); Nicholls; Fletcher; Arthur Wenban (Milton Regis), **F:** Registry closed 1947, housebarge 1934, at Pin Mill until c.1960, then hulked and broken up.

Florence, **PoR:** Faversham, **ON:** 20689, **YB:** 1858, **WB:** Murston, **B:** George Smeed, **RT:** 39, **O:** George Smeed Sittingbourne); Smeed Dean & Co. (Sittingbourne), **F:** Buried into Marsh Berth, Murston, c.1914.

Francis (Later *Fanny Maria*), **PoR:** Rochester, **ON:** 49827, **YB:** 1864, **WB:** Milton, **B:** Charles Burley, **RT:** 44, **O:** Charles Burley (Sittingbourne); Mrs. Clara R.Burley (Borden), **F:** Derelict 1939, broken up at Dolphin Yard, Sittingbourne 1979.

Fred, **PoR:** Rochester, **ON:** 84385, **YB:** 1881, **WB:** Murston, **B:** Smeed Dean & Co., **RT:** 44, **O:** H.Covington (London); Smeed Dean & Co.(Sittingbourne); Higgs, **F:** Became a lighter, broken up at Kettles Hard, Chatham, in 1975.

George, **PoR:** Rochester, **ON:** 81851, **YB:** 1879, **WB:** Murston, **B:** Smeed Dean & Co., **RT:** 43, **O:** Smeed Dean & Co. (Sittingbourne), **F:** Hulked at Conyer, broken up c.1966.

Gordon, **PoR:** London, **ON:** 91992, **YB:** 1887, **WB:** Battersea, **B:** Uncertain, but Robert Miller likely, **RT:** 40, **O:** Robert Miller (Battersea).

Gore Court, **PoR:** Rochester, **ON:** 84429, **YB:** 1882, **WB:** Murston, **B:** Smeed Dean & Co., **RT:** 45, **O:** Smeed Dean & Co. (Sittingbourne); Thomas Schmidt (Queenborough), **F:** Housebarge at Conyer, broken up 1970.

Harry, **PoR:** London, **ON:** 56922, **YB:** 1868, **WB:** Conyer, **B:** John Bird, **RT:** 28, **O:** Henry Millichamp & Co. (Conyer); Osborn Dan (Faversham); Frederick Bunting (Faversham).

Iverna, **PoR:** Harwich, **ON:** 91340, **YB:** 1892, **WB:** Sandwich, **B:** Felton, **RT:** 68, **O:** Holmes; John Wilks (Deal); Samuel West (Gravesend), F: Clubhouse for Greenwich Yacht Club, broken up.

John Bright, **PoR:** Rochester, **ON:** 76611, **YB:** 1877, **WB:** Sittingbourne, **B:** Not known, **RT:** 42, **O:** Smeed Dean & Co. (Sittingbourne).

Kent, **PoR:** Faversham, **ON:** 28452, **YB:** 1860, **WB:** Sittingbourne, **B:** George Smeed, **RT:** 35, **O:** George Smeed (Sittingbourne); Smeed Dean & Co. (Sittingbourne).

Leonard Piper, **PoR:** London, **ON:** 129071, **YB:** 1910, **WB:** East Greenwich, **B:** James R.Piper, **RT:** 99, **O:** James R.Piper (East Greenwich); Thomas Scholey; Samuel West & Co. (London); **F:** Auxiliary 1934, housebarge at Chiswick.

Livingstone, **PoR:** Rochester, **ON:** 81883, **YB:** 1880, **WB:** Murston, **B:** Smeed Dean & Co., **RT:** 44, **O:** Smeed Dean & Co. (Sittingbourne); A.Smith.

Mary, **PoR:** London(1), Rochester(2), Faversham(3), **ON:** 11275, **YB:** 1819, **WB:** Hammersmith, **B:** Not known, **RT:** 29 (67 tons deadweight capacity on first Register), **O:** Original owner(s) not known; John & Michael Lock (Gillingham); Edward Ashenden (Bobbing); John Hills (Milton Regis); Smeed Dean & Co. (Murston), **F:** Broken up and Registry closed 1898.

Perseverance, **PoR:** Rochester, **ON:** 9120, **YB:** 1824, **WB:** London, **B:** Not known, **RT:** 40, **O:** John Huggens; Smeed Dean & Co. (Sittingbourne); Brasier.

Persevere, **PoR:** Rochester, **ON:** 94572, **YB:** 1889, **WB:** Murston, **B:** Smeed Dean & Co., **RT:** 44, **O:** Smeed Dean & Co. (Sittingbourne); Theobald (Leigh); M.Maynard (Brightlingsea); Peter Carey (Gt. Wakering), **F:** Motor barge 1946, housebarge at Conyer, broken up 2007.

S.D., **PoR:** London, **ON:** 114831, **YB:** 1902, **WB:** Murston, **B:** Smeed Dean & Co., **RT:** 99, **O:** Smeed Dean & Co. (Sittingbourne); Marshall, **F:** Sunk by U-Boat 18 miles N.N.W. of Cape Antifer, France on 02/08/1916.

Swiftsure, **PoR:** Rochester, **ON:** 58434, **YB:** 1867, **WB:** Halling, **B:** George Higham, **RT:** 39, **O:** William Weekes & George Higham (Halling); Samuel Smith (Halling); William Lee & Sons (Halling); George G.Scott (Chelmondiston); Marsland; Gillett (Faversham); W.Peacock, **F:** By 1930s housebarge at Otterham, hulked 1940s and part buried/broken up there.

Valonia, **PoR:** Rochester, **ON:** 132631, **YB:** 1911, **WB:** East Greenwich, **B:** Shrubsall, **RT:** 90, **O:** T.Middleton (Harwich); Horace Shrubsall (Greenwich), **F:** In collision with tanker *Limousin*, 1940, declared Constructive Total Loss.

Venta (Ex. *Jachin*), **PoR:** London, **ON:** 96486, **YB:** 1893, **WB:** Maldon, **B:** John T.Howard, **RT:** 70, **O:** Horace Shrubsall (Limehouse); Miss E.Shrubsall (Blackheath); Alice Shrubsall (Blackheath); Harvey (Rochester); William Rice; Judge Blagden; Nicholas Hardinge; Jocelyn Lukins; Paul Goldsack, **F:** Yacht by 1947, sailed to Sweden 1964, returned to England 1966 and was berthed on the Thames opposite Battersea Power Station until towed to Aylesford, River Medway, in 1985 as housebarge, moved to Cuxton where caught fire and burnt out November 5th 1991.

Victoria, **PoR:** London, **ON:** 108233, **YB:** 1897, **WB:** Sittingbourne, **B:** Alfred White, **RT:** 54, **O:** Henry Austen; Smeed Dean & Co. (Sittingbourne); E.J.Butcher; Ellis (Sittingbourne); Wrinch (Erwarton); Andrews (Bradfield), F: Housebarge by 1950, hulked at Bradfield, Essex, by 1977.

Vincent, **PoR:** Rochester, **ON:** 79879, **YB:** 1879, **WB:** Murston, **B:** Smeed Dean & Co., **RT:** 35, **O:** Smeed Dean & Co. (Sittingbourne), **F:** Sold c.1930, became roads barge at East Greenwich, then broken up.

Whitehall, **PoR:** Rochester, **ON:** 84399, **YB:** 1881, **WB:** Murston, **B:** Smeed Dean & Co., **RT:** 37, **O:** Smeed Dean & Co. (Sittingbourne), **F:** derelict at Northfleet by 1947.

William & Sarah, **PoR:** Faversham, **ON:** 11992, **YB:** 1838, **WB:** King's Arms Stairs (Surrey), **B:** Not known, **RT:** 35, **O:** George Smeed (Sittingbourne); Smeed Dean & Co. (Sittingbourne), **F:** Sold 1880s.

Winnie, **PoR:** Rochester, **ON:** 81896, **YB:** 1880, **WB:** Murston, **B:** Smeed Dean & Co., **RT:** 45, **O:** Smeed Dean & Co. (Sittingbourne); A.Smith, **F:** derelict at Rushenden, Isle of Sheppey, broken up 1940.

Wyvenhoe, **PoR:** London, **ON:** 110012, **YB:** 1898, **WB:** Wivenhoe, **B:** Forrestt & Co., **RT:** 63, **O:** Augustus George Hughes (Greenwich); Tilbury Contracting & Dredging Co. (London); John George Hammond (London); London & Rochester Barge Co. (Rochester); London & Rochester Trading Co. (Rochester); Frank A.G. & Mrs.J.Kennedy (Rochester); Payne's Marine Transport (Queenborough); Oatside Ltd. (Enfield); Wyvenhoe (London) Ltd. (Enfield); Kemira Coatings Ltd. (Haverhill); Charisma Consultants Ltd. (London); **F:** Converted from sail to motor-barge 1923, restored to sail 1982.

Young Jack, **PoR:** Rochester, **ON:** 81884, **YB:** 1880, **WB:** Murston, **B:** Smeed Dean & Co., **RT:** 44, **O:** Smeed Dean & Co. (Sittingbourne); McDermott, F: Registry closed 08/02/1932, hulked then buried at Stoke Saltings.

Of the thirty-nine barges listed here just one, the *Wyvenhoe*, survives under active sail. She is available for sailing charters for up to twelve passengers, based on the River Blackwater. The *Leonard Piper* is seeing out her days as a houseboat at Chiswick. None of the others survive complete, though for some, the locations where they were finally hulked to rot away have been recorded by the Society for Sailing Barge Research in the Society publication Last Berth of the Sailorman.

APPENDIX B - STRIKE LETTER

Transcript of a letter from the Rev. Robert Payne Smith, Chaplain at Milton Vicarage, dated April 18th 1890, in reply to that sent from the Archbishop of Canterbury's office of April 17th 1890, by the Rt. Rev. St. Clair George Alfred Donaldson, on behalf of Archbishop Edward White Benson, regarding the bargemen's strike. Punctuation is left as written. The letter was located at, and is reproduced here with the permission of, Lambeth Palace Library.

Milton Vicarage
Sittingbourne
April 18.90

My dear Sir

In reply to your letter of April 17 received this evening I think I had better tell you how things have gone here.

About the middle of Feb: last the Bargemens Union for these waters - Faversham to Rochester - framed a 'list of prices' for the brick trade & sent it to the employers with the note that it would come into effect on March 1st.

The Barges trade at per freight per journey - 1/2 going to barge owner 1/2 to Captain & Mate.

The men say that the freights were reduced some years back and that they were promised that the old prices should be restored when the state of the Brick trade permitted, that the time had come and that it was only when individual appeals had been useless that the Union formulated its claim.

On the other side the Masters 1st. object to the actual manner in which the 'List' was presented to them & certainly it was presented more like a highwaymans pistol than like an appeal for extra wages & 2nd. they declare that the actual state of trade renders it impossible for them to pay all asked.

The actual Strike began March 1st. on the Masters refusing to pay the new list.

On hearing that the Strike would cause the Brickmakers to be 'locked out' Messrs Venn, Freeman, Hanham & myself sent a joint note to the Chairman of the Masters Union suggesting that the dispute with the bargemen might well be settled by some form of conciliation or arbitration. We received a civil answer but it practically stated that the Masters could manage their own business & would not be dictated to by their men, by a Union or by outsiders - though they were ready at any time to take back their men on the old terms.

Since then negotiations have been going on continually & at the present moment the men have withdrawn their lists & the Masters have prepared new ones which will soon be considered. There is a general impression that the strike will soon be over, but I rather question if the wire pullers will allow the Union to yield at all.

So much has been said one side & the other that I fear Masters & Men are thinking more about a nominal victory than about the practical interests involved. In fact the whole question has been treated here as if it were a totally new matter & neither side seem to have gained any experience from what has very plainly been taught by the history of all strikes - vis: the mutual injury to capital & labour.

I suggest with great diffidence that if His Grace were to write & urge Masters & Men to meet each other on some footing of mutual give & take it might prove the golden bridge to somewhat overheated personal feeling & enable either side to retreat from untenable positions too hurriedly taken up.

Mr G E Wragge, 47 Belvedere Road, Lambeth is Sec: to the Masters Union.

Mr C F Ashton, Rochester is Sec: to the Bargemens Soc:

This if matters do not end tomorrow - about which I will write at once.

As regards the actual distress. The Lock Out has thrown a very large number of people out of work but it must be remembered that these very persons would probably be on strike now or a month or so hence had the Masters given in at once to the Bargemen.

Some weeks back a general committee for the relief of all irrespective of sect was formed in Sittingbourne - Mr Venn being Chairman. I regret I could not join it as I think those who hold official position in the Church have no right to throw their weight & influence one side or the other in these wretched disputes between Labour & Capital which if to be decided permanently for the benefit of the county must be decided in accordance with the absolute Laws of political economy.

And I am inclined to think that the help already given has tended to prolong the struggle. I understand that now the Committee has expended all its funds which may aid to end the Strike.

We have here helped our own Church people fairly liberally. The rest I consider have no claim on our alms.

But as a matter of fact we have as yet had no single application at the Workhouse for outdoor relief under labour test for which we have made provision so that what the 'anon' letter says about starvation & turnips is somewhat exagerated.

I return to the letter. I think from the writing & style that it comes from a ³/4 witted woman of fair education who has lately paraded with the processions of Bargees & Brickmakers etc and is entitled in the newspaper reports The Lady Standard Bearer.

I hope to go to town on Monday Evening for a day or two & could come down to Addington & talk the matter over with you or Mr Baynes if His Grace thought fit.

You must pardon so long and discussive an answer but I could not well make it shorter.

> *Believe me*
> > *Yours very truly*
> > > *R Payne Smith*

P.S. My address after Monday
> > *10 York Gate*
> > > *Regents Park*
> > > > *N.W:*

The Rev St. Clair Donaldson.

APPENDIX C - SMEED DEAN LETTERS

The content of twenty-four letters addressed to George Winn (includes one to Rose Winn) from Smeed Dean & Co., sent between 21st April 1906 and 5th January 1912 are transcribed here. Most were hand-written, as those which are reproduced on pages 95 and 96, on letterheads once bound into a pad with perforations on the left side of the page. A few are typed onto conventional letterheads. Those hand written are all signed or initialled by George Andrews, those typed include letters bearing a signature G. Andrews rubber stamped on his behalf, two bear the initials S.J.E. and one is initialled J.H.D. (John Hambrook Dean). All letters are from the Winn family collection.

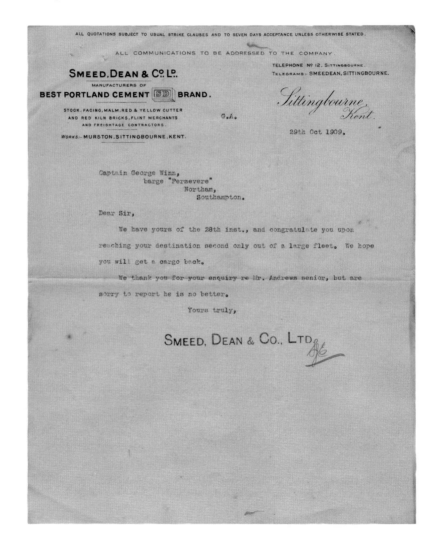

Text of letter dated April 21st 1906 to Mr. G Winn, Goodnestone Road, Sittingbourne:

Dear Sir,

I am indeed sorry because of your loss - it must be a severe blow to both yourself & your dear wife especially in her weak condition.

Will you please accept my sincere sympathy & also the sympathy of other members of this Company with you both in your bereavement - thank God his grace is always sufficient for as our day so even shall our strength be.

Anything you wish done please let me know. I shall be only too pleased to help you in any way.

Yours Truly, for Smeed Dean & Co. Ld.
    G. Andrews, Director

Text of letter dated November 3rd 1906 to Captain George Winn, Barge *Persevere*, Medina Wharf, Cowes:

Sir

We have your letter. I do not in any way blame you for the wet cement.

We of course wish it had not happened - make the best of it & bring back all that is damaged.

We thought you would have stopped at Dover on Saturday night, the wind backing & falling light & glass low - but the manner in which you have navigated the barge & sheltered her & ridden her is worthy of praise & we shall look upon you as our first Coaster.

We must of course make the barge seaworthy in stress of weather.

Yours Truly, Smeed Dean & Co. Ld. G.A.

P.S. You cannot very well look for a back freight as you will have cement in - empty out all partly damaged & fill as many sacks as you can.

Text of letter dated February 5th 1907 to Captain G. Winn, Barge *Persevere*, Medina Wharf, Cowes, I. of W.:

Sir,

Your letter received - we will have the barge on the blocks when you return & see if we can find out where the trouble is - it is probably weakness in the runs -

Crundall's have a cargo of Pitch pine stowable stuff ex Steamer at Southampton for Folkstone & offer 4/6 load and 21/- gratuity.

I have agreed nothing as it depends upon barge & Steamer being ready together & I believe Steamer was due in Yesterday - You might go over to Southampton to Crundalls office & ascertain about the fit & fix if you wish.

Yours Truly, Smeed Dean & Co Ld, GA

Text of letter dated February 20th 1907 to Captain G. Winn,
Barge *Persevere*, Torquay:

Sir

> *We think you did well in getting down as quickly as you did.*
> *Be careful & let us know what you are doing for a freight back.*
> *We have tried in London but cannot grt* anything suitable to*
offer for you.
> *Yours Truly, Smeed Dean & Co Ld   GA*

* *grt* - Abbreviated form of guarantee.

Text of letter dated August 23rd 1907 to Captain G. Winn,
Barge *Persevere*, Loading Oak Timber, Surrey Commercial Docks,
London, S.E.:

Sir,

> *Yours of the 22nd inst. to hand. The cost of loading Timber*
comes out of the freight. The charge used to be 1/6 per load, so that if
you have got it done for 8d., you have done very well.
> *The Timber will be taken out at Dover by crane free of expense.*
> *Yours truly, For Smeed, Dean & Co. Ld.*
> *G.Andrews, Director.*

Text of letter dated November 7th 1907 to Captain G. Winn,
Barge *Persevere*, Folkstone:

Sir,

> *Your letter of date received. Sorry you have a long day - Note*
damage or collision - do not report.
> *We are busy with Essex Coaster Work just now so come direct*
home if nothing special offering when you are unloaded.
> *Yours Truly, Smeed Dean & Co Ld   G.A.*

Text of letter dated November 26th 1907 to Captain G. Winn,
Barge *Persevere*, Dover:

Sir

> *Would you care to go to Exmouth from our Cement Works with a*
full freight of Cement at 6/- & one guinea gratuity free of brokerage.
> *If so come direct home as we can load quickly - don't take it if you*
would rather not go down Channel so far this winter - do please decide for
yourself & oblige as we wish you to do what you yourself think best.
> *Please telephone us between 9. & 10 tomorrow Wednesday.*
> *Yours Truly, Smeed Dean & Co Ld   GA*

Text of letter dated December 17th 1907 to Captain G. Winn,
c/o Mr. G. Draper, Cowes:

Sir

We enclose B/Lading* and fresh Transire.**

We hope you will get unloaded quickly & reach home in time to load before Xmas -

You were very plucky to ride out the terrific gale on Friday. We all wondered wherever you were & how you were getting on.

Very many craft came to grief up & down the coast.

You will load for Exmouth & get down as soon as ever possible.

Yours Truly, Smeed Dean & Co Ld   GA

2 enc.

* *B/Lading* - Abbreviated form of Bill of Lading.

** *Transire* - An account to be delivered in duplicate by a coastwise vessel's master, before departure, detailing goods laden. One copy, once signed becomes the vessel's clearance. On arrival at the port of discharge, the Transire must be delivered to the port collector within 24 hours and before discharge.

Text of letter dated January 6th 1908 to Captain G. Winn,
Barge *Persevere*, Exmouth:

Sir

Your wire received. We are glad you have arrived. It has been very rough today wind S.W.

Can you get sails repaired at Exmouth?

We Shall no doubt get a letter from you giving particulars of damage to sails.

You have to unload at Exmouth Dock

Try & get a freight back.

Yours Truly, Smeed Dean & Co Ld   GA

Text of letter dated January 8th 1908 to Captain G. Winn,
Barge *Persevere*, Exmouth:

Sir

We have your letter & note what you state about the sails - get done what is necessary at Exmouth.

The weather keeps very bad - the barges that were with you at Faversham have not yet got round the Foreland yet & some of the Essex barges are not unloaded.

Hope you will get fixed for a good freight back.

Yours Truly, Smeed Dean & Co Ld   GA

Text of letter dated January 9th 1908 to Captain G. Winn, Barge
Persevere, c/o Mr. G. Draper, Cowes, I. of W.:

Sir

*Your letter to hand. You had better buy a jib if you can get a
suitable one cheap & probably you can.*

As to C.C. the old one is of use for 21 days but you will no
doubt be asked for a new one at Cowes*

*As Harold does not know the particulars of crew you had
perhaps better get a Cowes Broker to get a new C.C. for you.*

Wind fresh N.E. here tonight - how changeable it is.

Yours Truly, Smeed Dean & Co Ld   GA

* *C.C.* - Clearance Certificate which listed crew members, for coasting
vessels under 200 Reg. Tons. It was a 'running' document, recording
engagement and discharge of crew members, and was valid for six months.

Text of letter dated January 27th 1908 to Captain G. Winn, *Persevere*:

Sir

*Mr Such has just telephoned us offering a full freight of Oil
Cake at 6/6 & one guinea to load at Wandsworth for Kingsbridge -*

You can decide for yourself if you will take it or not.

*We want a barge to load 110 tons Cement for Plymouth 5/6 &
21/- gratuity - if you care to do this you can load coke home.*

Let us know at once as Mr Such is waiting for us to telephone him -

*Please understand you can quite please yourself if you will go
down Channel again with Persevere - I wanted to speak to you this mg*
but you were gone.*

Yours Truly, Smeed Dean & Co Ld   GA

* Presumed abbreviation for *morning*.

Text of letter dated March 21st 1909 to Mrs. Winn:

Dear Mrs Winn,

*I have received a letter from your husband & I am not replying
to him but to you to ask you please to see that he does what his doctor
advises -*

*It is particularly important that he does not take any risks & you
will do both ourselves & your husband a favour by keeping him very
quiet & obedient.*

*If I had known he was unwell last time I would not have allowed
him to leave.*

*Tell him please I will see that the barge is in proper hands for a
trip & hope he will soon fully recovered.*

Yours Truly, Smeed Dean & Co Ld   G Andrews

Text of letter dated September 13th 1909 to Captain G. Winn, Barge *Persevere*, alongside S.S. *Queen Wilhelmina*, Surrey Commercial Docks, London, S.E.:

Dear Sir,

    Your letter of the 11th inst. received.

    I am glad to get your letter but you must try to avoid worry, it does no good & may do much harm. It will be my pleasure to talk to you when next at home & to arrange for you to have a short rest if you really need it -

    We all need to learn to live one day at a time "Give us this day our daily bread" and for you to keep at sea so long without rest is wrong & in the end may do more harm than good - May God ever keep & bless you & your wife & family.

    Yours Truly, Geo. Andrews.

Text of letter dated September 17th 1909 to Captain G. Winn, Barge *Persevere*, Dover:

Sir

    Enclosed is transire, fill in date at back.

    Try & get something away, things are very slack here .

    Let us know what you are doing, hope you are feeling better.

    Yours Truly, Smeed Dean & Co Ld   GA

Text of letter dated October 26th 1909 to Captain G. Winn, Barge *Persevere*, Southampton:

Dear Sir

    Very glad indeed to hear of your safe arrival.

    It was a terribly rough time Friday night last - Hope can get a freight back.

    Yours Truly, Smeed Dean & Co Ld   GA

Text of letter dated October 29th 1909 to Captain G. Winn, Barge *Persevere*, Northam, Southampton:

Dear Sir

    We have yours of the 28th inst., and congratulate you upon reaching your destination second only out of a large fleet. We hope you will get a cargo back.

    We thank you for your enquiry re Mr. Andrews senior, but are sorry to report he is no better.

    Yours Truly, Smeed, Dean & Co., Ltd.   SJE

Text of letter dated November 8th 1910 to Mr George Winn, Bargeman, Inpatient, Seamans Hospital, Greenwich:

Dear Captain
> *We are much concerned at the news that you have to go in the hospital & shall be glad to know what is the matter with you.*
> *I shall call & see you as soon as possible & meantime can pray that you may speedily recover.*
> *Will let the mate bring the barge home with coke & then go on the ways.**
> *Yours Truly, Smeed Dean & Co Ld   G. Andrews*

* Ways - an abbreviation for slipway.

Text of letter dated May 12th 1911 to Captain G. Winn, Barge *Persevere*, Newport, I. of W.:

Dear Sir
> *Messrs Crundalls inform us now that there is only a few loads over, one fix* of lumber** for Ipswich from Southampton & therefore they have nothing to offer us back at the moment for your barge.*
> *We hope you will get fixed up quickly & that your present cargo will turn out right.*
> *Yours Truly, Smeed Dean & Co Ld   GA*

* Fix - Freights are 'fixed' for a vessel.
** Lumber - Sawn timber.

Text of letter dated September 16th 1911 to Captain G. Winn, Barge *Persevere*, Ealing, Nr. Southampton:

Dear Sir,
> *We have yours of the 15th inst., and note your safe arrival.*
> *Messrs. W. Crundall & Co., of Dover inform us they have a freight of timber to go from Southampton to Shoreham. Please therefore get into touch with their Southampton Office and endeavour to fix this up, and oblige. Let us know what you are doing,*
> *Yours Truly, Smeed, Dean & Co., Ltd.   J.H.D.*

Text of letter dated October 30th 1911 to Capt. G. Winn, Barge
Persevere, C/o Harbour Master, Shoreham, Sussex:

Dear Sir
*   Your letter of the 28th inst. is to hand. You must have had a*
terrible time on Thursday; the weather has been so catchy. Last week the
glass was low with occasional fine weather but to-day it is fairly high
and blowing half a gale of wind. You will be glad to know the Gertrude
May has reached home safe although in a very leaky state. She had a
hard hammering on the beach and old Tom has got his face and arm
bruised, but nothing serious.
*   You will of course do exactly as you please respecting Besent's*
offer. The Maria finished loading Barley at Newport on Saturday, and
expected to leave; I am rather anxious about him; he is bound to Whitstable.
*   Yours Truly, Smeed, Dean & Co., Ltd.   G. Andrews*

Text of letter dated December 4th 1911 to Capt. G. Winn, Barge
Persevere, Newport, I. of W.:

Dear Sir
*   We have your wire & hope you will finish on Wednesday so as to*
be able to get back in time to load cement here this week for St. Helens
at 5/-.
*   The Maria was fixed for timber last week & we cannot transfer the*
Charter & I do not care to send George Smeed down although she will
certainly go if you cannot get back in time to get down & cleared before Xmas.
*   Yours Truly, Smeed Dean & Co Ld   G Andrews*

Text of letter dated December 21st 1911 to Capt. G. Winn, Barge
Persevere, C/o Post Office, Dover.:

Dear Sir
*   We have yours of date & note your report of a strain.*
*   As to getting down Channel. We certainly should be please if it*
was possible to get down before the holidays but if you cannot make a
start then bring the barge into the inner harbour & we will pay the dues
& come home & spend the Christmas with you wife & family.
*   We know you richly deserve the time at home.*
*   Yours Truly, Smeed Dean & Co Ld   G Andrews*

Text of letter dated Jan 5th 1912 to Capt. G. Winn, Barge *Persevere*, C/o
Post Office, St. Helens, Isle-of-Wight.:

Dear Sir
*   We have your letter of the 4th inst., and are glad to note your safe*
arrival. We enclose herewith M.O. value £10 on account of freightage;
please acknowledge receipt. Mr J. Besent, Shipbroker, of 41, Great Tower
Street, E.C. appears to be anxious to get into touch with you. We have
informed him that you have arrived at St. Helens and no doubt you will
hear from him in due course if he has any business to offer you.
*   Yours Truly, Smeed, Dean & Co., Ltd.   SJE.*

APPENDIX D - POSTCARDS

Reproduced here are two of many postcards sent to family members from ports around England, the Channel Islands and the north French coast. These are from George Charles Winn, George Winn's eldest surviving son, to his sister Esther, at home in Sittingbourne during W.W.I. The first was post-marked 17th April 1916 when he was with his father in the *S.D.*, the second post-marked 18th August 1917, when he was in the *Leonard Piper*.

Posted in Cherbourg, from the *S.D.*, the text reads 'Barge SD, Cherbourg. My Dear Sister, just a line hoping it finds you quite well as it leaves us at present. We leave to-day for Alderney if there is a fair wind. Hope to see you soon. Hope mum & Norman are alright. All this time from your loving bro' George. x x x x x' George Charles Winn's brother Norman was eight years old at the time, having been born to Rose in her thirty-eighth year.

The Cherbourg postcard picture celebrates the nursing of war casualties with a caption which translated reads 'The Dream of the Wounded'. The illustration is a sepia photograph with the text, the crosses on the nurse's uniform, the injured man's blanket and the posy of flowers, all tinted by hand in appropriate colours.

DIEPPE. — Le Petit Baigneur récalcitrant.   ND. Phot.

The second postcard was sent from Dieppe in August 1917 when the British were fighting the German army in the Ypres trenches, just 100 miles away. Entitled 'Dieppe - The obstinate Little Swimmer', George Charles' text reads 'Leonard Piper, Sunday. Dear Esther, Just a card hoping you are all well & a good girl, look out for yourself if you are not when I get back. Hope to soon be back, from your loving bro' George. x x x' Note that George Charles had, by this time changed to 'Angleterre' instead of 'England' for the Winn family home address, perhaps an indication of his increasing familiarity with the local language following many trips to French ports.

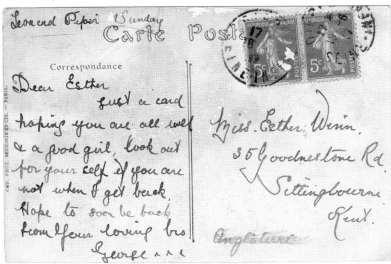

APPENDIX E - JOHN WILKS LETTERS

The content of seventeen hand-written letters addressed to Mr. G. Winn, Capt. CB "Leonard Piper" 15 Ramuz Drive, Westcliff on Sea, Essex, from John Wilks, owner of the *Leonard Piper* and other barges at the time. 'CB' would have been an abreviation similar to the more familiar 'SB' for 'Sailing Barge', probably standing for 'Coasting Barge'. The first letter is dated 14th October 1920, the last 6th April 1921. Fifteen were written in an eleven week period between mid-January and early April 1921. Words <u>underlined</u> are uncertain. All letters are from the Winn family collection.

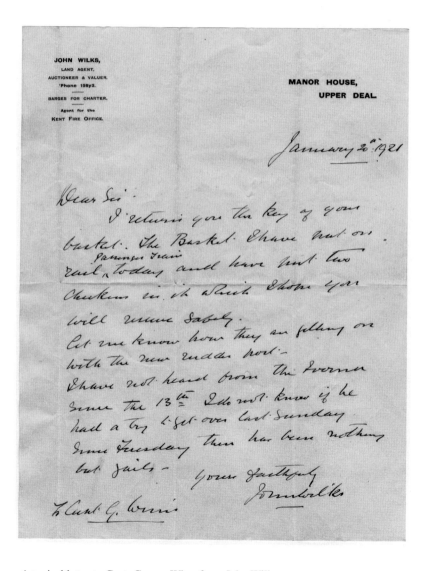

A typical letter to Capt. George Winn from John Wilks.

Text of letter dated October 14th 1920.

Dear Sir

Yours to hand. I will see you about the tax.

You will not make any return for 1920 & 1921 - until after the 31st of March 1921.

Think you will find you have made 1918 & 1919 on £1600 and for the years 1919 & 1920 on £1449 less all your expenses.

Then you will make your return for 1920 & 1921 after the 31st of March 1921 - but I will see you when you are in London.

Your seen hopping about like steam again, hope you will have good luck.

Yours faithfully, John Wilks

To Capt G Winn

Text of letter dated December 2nd 1920.

Dear Sir

Just received your wire, I have been thinking about you - you must have got a bit of a dusting. Glad to know you are in Port.

Yours faithfully, John Wilks

To Capt G Winn

Text of letter dated January 16th 1921.

Dear Sir

I thank you very much for the handsome present you have sent to my mother, and also for your letter - She is writing you a letter which is a bit of a business at her advanced age.

Will forward you on the key and basket by rail first chance I get.

Thanking you and Mrs Winn for your kind wishes.

Yours faithfully, John Wilks

To Capt G Winn

Text of letter dated January 20th 1921.

Dear Sir

I return to you the key of your basket I have put on rail Passenger Train today and have put two chickens in it which I hope you will receive safely.

Let me know how they are getting on with the new rudder post.

I have not heard from the Iverna* since the 13th. I do not know if he had a try to get over last Sunday. Since Tuesday there has been nothing but gails (sic.).

Yours faithfully, John Wilks

To Capt G Winn

*Iverna; spritsail barge built by Felton at Sandwich in 1892, Off. No. 91340, 68 tons, owned by John Wilks and skippered by George Charles Winn from 17th March 1920 having left his father and the *Leonard Piper* earlier in the month.

Text of letter dated January 26th 1921.

Dear Sir

Re. Iverna

Yours to hand - I am quite agreeable that if you can see Messrs John Holmans about the cancelled Charter with Iverna that you should do so, and I am certain your son will be glad if you will take it in hand for him.

Get the bill for your repairs and check it through and send it onto me - they have been a terrible long time over the job. When I had the new rudder post for Iverna & her new steering gear it was in <u>service</u> in under 8 days.

Yours faithfully, John Wilks

Text of letter dated January 27th 1921.

Dear Sir

Your letter & Wiggins' to hand by midday post.

I have written Wiggins that I'll not want the stern post interfered with to weaken it in any way.

The other way would be to make two big washers to take the bearing or to make two fresh gudgeons irons & put on the stern post. We do not want the stern post damaged too much. Please write & let me know what you are doing with it. It must have a bearing on all the gudgeons.

Yours faithfully, John Wilks

To Capt G Winn

PS. Have not heard from the Iverna - Don't you have my stern post split about so as to weaken the ship.

Text of letter dated January 31st 1921.

Dear Sir

Your accounts to hand and notes value £4-0-0 to balance up freight.

Let me know how the new Rudder Post acts when you write.

Yours faithfully, John Wilks

To Capt G Winn

Text of letter dated February 22nd 1921.

Dear Sir
> *Your Wire to hand. When you get discharged I am going to have the work on the new Rudder post surveyed.*
> *Let me know at who's wharf you are discharging and what cargo you have brought over - I will come up when we arrange for the survey, so will Messrs. Cole & Wiggins.*
> *Sorry to inform you that C. Winn is not getting on at all well with the Iverna - He always has troubles. He states his wife is ill & he had to go to Faversham but I am loosing my confidence in him and shall not have much more of it. Possibly you know by now some of his troubles.*
> *Mr. Shrubsall will make the Survey for me so get in touch with him on the phone - and if neccessary we must put the barge on the blocks - and give me if possible two days notice - If you have any complaints about the working of the rudder please write me a letter to that effect.*
> *Yours faithfully, John Wilks*
To Capt G Winn
PS I understood yesterday they were giving 13/6 <u>Carteret</u>* to Sandwich, Stone. Mr. Shrubsall may not want the barge on the blocks. JW.

* *Carteret* - A small harbour to the west of Cherbourg.

Text of first letter dated February 28th 1921.

Dear Sir
> *I have agreed with Messrs Cole & Wiggins to fit the collars on the rudder post & to be fitted to my satisfaction. So when convenient please have it done & write me if they make a good job of it.*
> *With regards to the Charter of the Iverna to Yersche* for Shell, I shall be seeing Holman in the course of a few days, and will see what they say about it. I shall not go into any litigation myself, or as owner, on the matter as it would mean the Lawyers taking the barge & possibly a lot of expense.*
> *No letter from C. Winn. Things are most unsatisfactory in that quarter. I have written him today and also the brokers at Cowes - If you have any news of him please let me know - if you have.*
> *Yours faithfully, John Wilks*
To Capt G Winn

*Yersche - A small port on the Ooster Sheldte waterway in Holland.

Text of second letter dated February 28th 1921.

Dear Sir
> *I received wire by midday that Iverna arrived at Cherbourg this morning. So the young man has made a start again.*
> *Yours faithfully, John Wilks*
To Capt G Winn

Text of letter dated March 2nd 1921.

Dear Sir

> *Your accounts to hand with cheque value £50-0-0.*
> *You state that you had 180$^1/_2$ tons   £135-7-6*
> *I understood you had 190 tons   £142-10-0*
> *Please let me know if you have made a mistake.*
> *Thank you for the 20/- returned. Glad to hear you have*
> fixed. Let me know the Broker.*
> *Yours faithfully, John Wilks*

To Capt G Winn

Text of letter dated March 15th 1921.

Dear Sir

> *Your wire to hand fo which I thank you. Did not expect you back*
> so soon.*
> *Yours faithfully, John Wilks*

To Capt G Winn

Text of letter dated March 18th 1921.

Dear Sir

> *If I get a contract for Stone to Sandwich, what do you think would*
> be fair price from Cherbourg, Geurnsey or <u>Carteret</u>. Do you happen to*
> know any of the addresses of the Stone Merchants at these ports.*
> *Yours faithfully, John Wilks*

To Capt G Winn
'Private'
PS. I understand I am to be asked to tender.

Text of letter dated March 23rd 1921.

Dear Sir

> *I thank you for your accounts and cheque to balance £62-3-10*
> which seems quite correct.*
> *If you don't get fixed I should get Messrs Wests to give her sides*
> a coat of black.*
> *What does Cole & Wiggins say about fitting the washers on?*
> *Yours faithfully, John Wilks*

To Capt G Winn

Text of letter dated March 29th 1921.

Dear Sir

> *Your letter to hand for which I thank you. I don't quite understand it - if things are not satisfactory at West's*, we must find another spot. You proposed having her sides done there - do not blame me.*
> *Did they make a good job of the sail.*
> *Yours faithfully, John Wilks*

To Capt G Winn

* *West's* - Samuel West Ltd. built, rebuilt, repaired and maintained their own and other barges at Terrace Pier Wharf, Gravesend, now the site of the Port of London Authority headquarters.

Text of letter dated April 1st 1921

Dear Sir

> *I thank you for your letter. Mr. J.B. Hartley wrote this morning requesting me to send him an account for your earnings for next year's Income Tax. I have returned you for £966-8-2,*
> *And told him you had all your expenses to come out of this.*
> *Things are very bad now.*
> *Yours faithfully, John Wilks*

To Capt G Winn

Text of letter dated April 6th 1921

Dear Sir

> *I thank you for you letter and the report on the rudder which is satisfactory. I hope you will manage to fix up the cement & clay back.*
> *Yours faithfully, John Wilks*

To Capt G Winn

The tone of Wilks' letters to George Winn suggest that their relationship may have been strained by George's son, George Charles', performance with Wilk's *Iverna*, and further soured as time went by, the rather telling 'Do not blame me' in the letter of 29th March 1921, suggesting that all was not well between them. It is reasonable to assume that George's mind was already elsewhere, for it was just three months later that he purchased his first barge, the big Rye ketch *Diana*, and had probably been on the lookout for a suitable barge to skipper own, for some time.

The first two, and only surviving, pages from a log book of the *Askoy*, covering a winter passage from Southend to Antwerp, 25th November to 1st December 1925. From the Winn family collection.

Increasing To a Strong Gale
Two anchors down, & ——
draging, dangeriously To
leeward, Signlled, for assistance
riding heavyly,
75' Fathoms on First anchor,
& 50. Fathoms on The Second,
Takern out @ 1.30, P.M.
by. the margate life Boat,
Wind Moderating @
Midnight, Put back
on board, @ 9. a.m.
Nov 26.th "askoy" Strained
& Takern Water In,
Two feet Inholed,
Ingaged asistance To Pump,
Proceeded on Voyge To
antwerp, Nov 26.th @ 5. P.M.
Sheltered @ zeebrugge
Nov 27.th N.W. Gale,
arrived antwerp, ~~Nov~~ Dec 1.st

APPENDIX G - CHARTER-PARTIES

Abbreviated transcripts of Charter-Parties for *Askoy* and *Ethel Edith* raised between 1925 and 1928 by Giani & Muller, Shipbrokers, Antwerp and Harvie, Sons & Co., London. Text in italics is from written or typed copy within a standard pro-forma of the documents. From the Winn family collection.

SAIL F

GIANI & MULLER
SHIPBROKERS
ANTWERP
Telegrams: GIANI

CHARTER-PARTY

ANTWERP, *December 12th* 19*25*

It is this day mutually agreed between *the owner*
of the sailing vessel, *Askoy*
of ____ tons net register or thereabout, carrying *200* tons deadweight or thereabout
now *He passage to London*
and *Messrs. A. J. Suriq ~ Co Ltd* Charterers.

The said ship being tight, staunch and strong, and in every way fitted for the voyage, shall, with all convenient speed, after having discharged her inward cargo, proceed to a berth as ordered ~~in one of the Antwerp Docks~~ *at Terhaegen* and there load, for account of the said charterers, a full and complete cargo of *bricks*

not exceeding what she can reasonably stow and carry besides her tackle, apparel, provisions and furniture.

The ship being so loaded, shall proceed to *Southend on sea, corporation Jetty but if the weather is such that vessel cannot go to Southend, then she is to proceed to Sagenlam dock for discharging* or so near thereunto as she may safely get, and deliver the cargo, on being paid freight as follows: *8/3 eight shillings and three pence per ton if discharging at Southend or 8/- per ton if discharging at Sagenlam Dock, always with £2.2 - gratuity to the captain.*

The cargo to be put free in and taken free out of the vessel at merchant's risk and expense.

The freight to be paid in cash on unloading and right delivery of the cargo.
(The act of God, restraints of princes and rulers, the accidents of war, fire, ice, and all and every other dangers and accidents of the seas, rivers and navigation, of whatever nature and kind soever, during the said voyage, always mutually excepted). The usual negligence clause to apply to this charter.

The cargo to be loaded and discharged together within *six reversible working days*

Charterer is entitled to keep the vessel on demurrage, not exceeding ten days, at the rate of ____ per net register ton per day, payable day by day.

Advance, not exceeding one third of the freight to be allowed the Captain, if required, at port of loading, subject to insurance.

The owner or master to have an absolute lien upon the cargo for all freight, dead freight and demurrage.

The captain to sign bills of lading, *and/or* recharter, if required, at any rate of freight, without prejudice to this charter, if at less than chartered rate, difference to be paid before sailing, if at more, difference to be inserted as advance.

Merchant to pay all dues on the cargo.

A brokerage of five percent on all freight, deadfreight and demurrage is due by the vessel to **GIANI & MULLER**, on signment of this charter, vessel lost or not lost, charter cancelled or not cancelled and the vessel to be reported by them at the customhouse of ANTWERP, in and outwards, also on her first return, and by their agents at the ports of loading and discharge.

Average, if any, to be settled according York and Antwerp rules of ~~1890.~~ *1924*

Penalty for non-performance of this agreement, estimated amount of freight.

This charter is binding for consecutive voyages up to the end of March 1926 captain being at liberty to take each time cargo from U. K. to Continent. Shippers of the cargo: Gebroeders Lauduydt at Terlaegen.

For the Captain by authority sg. Giani ~ Muller as brokers

For A. J. Suriq ~ Co Ltd sg. Gruder Suriq Director

Full main text of Charter-Party dated *December 12th 1925* shown opposite.

It is this day mutually agreed between *the owner* of the sailing vessel, *Askoy* of ..... tons net register or thereabout, carrying *200* tons deadweight or thereabout now *on passage to London* and *Messrs. A. G. Surig & Co. Ltd* Charterers.

The said ship being tight, staunch and strong, and in every way fitted for the voyage, shall, with all convenient speed, after having discharged her inward cargo, proceed to a berth as ordered *at Terhaegen* and there load, for account of the said charterers, a full and complete cargo of *bricks* not exceeding what she can reasonably stow and carry besides her tackle, apparel, provisions and furniture.

The ship being so loaded, shall proceed to *Southend on Sea, Corporation Jetty but if the weather is such that vessel cannot go to Southend, then she is to proceed to Dagenham Dock for discharging* or so near thereunto as she may safely get, and deliver the cargo, on being paid freight as follows: *8/3 eight shillings and three pence per ton if discharging at Southend or 8/- per ton if discharging at Dagenham Dock, always with £2.2.-. gratuity to the captain.*

The cargo to be put free in and taken free out of the vessel at merchant's risk and expense.

The freight to be paid in cash on unloading and right delivery of the cargo.

The cargo to be loaded and discharged together within *six recersible working days*.

Charterer is entitled to keep the vessel on demurrage, not exceeding ten days, at the rate of *1/-* per net register ton per day, payable day by day.

Advance, not exceeding one third of the freight to be allowed the captain, if required, at port of loading, subject to insurance.

The owner or master to have an absolute lien upon the cargo for all freight, dead freight and demurrage.

The captain to sign bills of lading, and/or recharter, if required, at any rate of freight, without prejudice to this charter, if at less than chartered rate, difference to be paid before sailing, if at more, difference to be inserted as advance.

Merchant to pay all dues on the cargo.

A brokerage of five per cent on all freight, dead freight and demurrage is due by the vessel to **Gianni & Muller**, on signment of this charter, vessel lost or not lost, charter cancelled or not cancelled and the vessel to be reported by them at the customhouse of Antwerp, in and outwards, also on her first return, and by their agents at the ports of loading and discharge.

Average, if any, to be settled according to York and Antwerp rules 0f ~~1890~~ *1924*.

Penalty for non-performance of this agreement, estimated ammount of freight.

This charter is binding for consecutive voyages up to the end of March 1926, captain being at liberty to take each time cargo from U.K. to Continent. Shippers of the cargo:

Gebroeders Landuydt at Terhaegen.

For the Captain	*For A.G. Surig & Co. Ltd*
by Authority	*sg: Gurau Surig*
sg: Giani & Muller	*Director*
as brokers	

Abbreviated main text of Charter-Party dated *May 20th 1926:*

... between *Captain G.Winn*

... sailing vessel *Askoy*

... *200* tons deadweight

... now *left Southend on Sea, today light for Antwerp* and *Mr. Louis Van Regemortel as agents for* Charterers.

... ordered to *Rumpst or vicinity as ordered*

... shall proceed to *Southend on Sea*

... paid freight as follows: *7/9 say seven shillings and nine pence per ton of 20 cwt. with £.2.2.0. gratuity to the Master.*

... loaded and discharged within *six reversible working days.*

... brokerage of *²/3 of* five per cent ... to Giani & Muller ... *¹/3 of 5% to L. Van Regemortel!*

Charterer's agents at London for the clearance of this ship:-

By telegraphic authority of	*By Captain's authority*
charterer Mr. E. Linssen London	*sg: Giani & Muller.*
sg: L. Van Regemortel	
as agents only	

Abbreviated main text of Charter-Party dated *August 21st 1926:*

... between *Captain G.Winn*

... sailing vessel *Askoy*

... *200* tons deadweight

... now *at Southend, discharging* and *Mr. E. Linssen* Charterers.

... ordered to *Rumpst or vicinity* ... and there load ... *bricks*

... shall proceed to *Southend on Sea, Corporation Jetty as ordered*

... paid freight as follows: *7/9 seven shillings and nine pence per ton of 20 cwt. with two guineas gratuity to the Master.*

... loaded and discharged within *six reversible working days.*

... brokerage of five per cent ... to Giani & Muller ... *¹/3 of 5% to charterers.*

Agents at London, Mr. E.Linssen, 101 Leadenhall Street, EC3.

This charter is concluded for three consecutive trips, with liberty for the ship to take each time cargo on the way.

By authority of both parties.

sg: Giani & Muller

Abbreviated main text of Charter-Party dated *October 4th 1926:*

... between *Captain Winn*
... sailing vessel *Askoy*
... *200* tons deadweight
... now *on passage to Southend* and *Mr. E. Linssen* Charterers.
... ordered to *Rumpst or vicinity* ... and there load ... *bricks*
... shall proceed to *Southend on Sea, Corporation Jetty as ordered*
... paid freight as follows: *7/9 seven shillings and nine pence per ton of 20 cwt.*
with two guineas gratuity to the Master.
... loaded and discharged within *six reversible working days. Vessel to take*
her turn with other seagoing vessels, and time to count as soon as there is a
berth available at Southend.
... brokerage of five per cent ... to Giani & Muller ... *¹/3 of 5% to charterers.*
Agents at London: E. Linssen, 101 Leadenhall Street, EC3.
This charter is concluded for three consecutive trips, with liberty for the ship
to take each time cargo on the way.
By authority of both parties.
sg: Giani & Muller

Abbreviated main text of Charter-Party dated *19th April 1928:*

... between *Captain G.Winn*
... sailing vessel *Ethel Edith*
... *180* tons deadweight
... now *Thames ready to sail* and *Societe Commerciale du Calais of Calais*
Merchant.
... proceed to *Calais as ordered* and there load ... *roofing tiles in bulk, not less*
than 160 tons,
... to proceed to *Messrs Dixon & Cardus Wharf, below bridge, Northam,*
Southampton
... paid freight as follows: *7/6 (sevenshillingsandsixpence) per ton on not less*
than 160tons with 42/- gratuity to Captain.
... loaded and discharged within *six weather working* days.
... demurrage ... 9d. per gross reg ton *per day.*
... brokerage of five per cent ... to Harvie, Sons & Co [79 Mark Lane, London,
E.C.3.].
For & by authority of
Messrs. Societe Commerciale
du Calais   *(sgd) G. Winn*
(sgd) Harvie Sons & Co
as Agents only

PICTURE SOURCES

A formal list follows which indicates the immediate source of illustrations within this book, and in most cases their origins. Without amplification, this does little to credit those who have gone to considerable trouble to help find images, many of them concurrent with the period of the narrative, nor the efforts of those whose photographs did not ultimately end up in print. To all of you, my sincere thanks.

I have already made mention of the help given by Hugh Perks, and his willingness for me to use some illustrations from his book about Smeed Dean, 'George Bargebrick Esquire'. In combination with George Winn's story, the two now give a greater depth to our understanding of the world of Victorian industry and coastal transport. Much of the Blue Circle Industries' archive, from which the Smeed Dean material emanated has, in recent times, had a rather chequered history. Some of it sadly seems lost; not surprising as it has been moved from place to place following the firm's demise and takeover by French owners Lafarge. With the help of the Lafarge PR consultant, Daniel Daniels and Alison Nolan of Gravesend Library, I have been steered to Sandra Soder and John Oxford of the Gravesend Historical Society. Their laudable efforts to rescue and preserve on behalf of Lefarge Cement UK Plc, the Blue Circle archive, have thankfully yielded pictures for these pages.

Going back a few years in George Winn's life, we have the good fortune to learn that at the time his family lived in Chelsea, c.1870, the area was well recorded in early pioneer photography by James Hedderly. The enthusiasm of Katrina Presedo and Dave Walker at the Local Studies department at Kensington Central Library, where the Hedderly collection is housed, is every researcher's dream!

The Museum of London's brilliant Anna Sparham is forgiven for taking leave in the middle of this project to have her baby! Her colleague Sarah Williams continued the first rate help initiated by Anna. The Guildhall Library and the London Metropolitan Archive staff have all been most helpful in organising illustrations. Noreen Marshall of the V&A, Ian Brown of Swanage Coastguard, Tug at www.thamestugs.co.uk, Oxford County Council Photograhic Archive, the National Maritime Museum Collection and Clare Brown of the Lambeth Palace Library have all played their part. Special thanks for pictures to Peter Morgan and his helpers at the Sittingbourne Heritage Museum; well worth a visit.

A significant source has been the Society for Sailing Barge Research Archive. The Society's involvement in the project has also nurtured a benevolent response from some of the commercial picture libraries, which have sharpened their pencils to provide images which would otherwise have been unaffordable for a focus interest publication such as this. In particular I record the help of the Bridgeman Art Library, Cabinet UK Limited, Tess Watts at the Mary Evans Photo Library, home of the Illustrated London News archive, Vince Chin of NetXPosure Design, Ken Beken at Beken of Cowes and Andrew Dunn, a freelance professional photographer, par excellence.

A number of individual sailing barge enthusiasts have contributed photos from their personal collections for which I express my thanks. Amongst 'the usual suspects' are Ray Rush, Tony Farnham and Bob Ratcliffe. New providers include David Jordan from his family photo collection, Trevor Edwards' collection of Sheppey postcards and Margaret Thompson of Wadebridge in Cornwall, via John Buckingham of Padstow Museum. To these I will add Andrew Clarke whose father Ronald took photographs of barges, excursion steamers, sailing ships and yachts in the 1930s.

Many letters and documents, as well as photographs and postcards, directly associated with George Winn, have been provided by his family. I am quite sure they had not fully realised the historical importance of their forbear's collection. David Juniper, George's grandson, Jo Drake and Maggie Kenwick, both great-grand-daughters, have provided a lot of material reproduced here, and their ongoing committment to answer questions along the way, made my task much the easier.

Thanks again to all the above mentioned and any others inadvertantly missed.

Richard Walsh

Where the word Photo appears, the name which follows is that of the photographer. At least, the provider is identified, current source listed last. Sources are listed by page number and position.

Front cover: Photo, J. Manning, Southend-on-Sea, Winn Family Collection; 9: Winn Family Collection; 10, 12, 13, 14, 15: Photos, James Hedderly, Royal Borough of Kensington & Chelsea Library; 16: Photo, Henry Taunt, Oxford County Council Photographic Archive; 17: Photo, James Hedderly, Royal Borough of Kensington & Chelsea Library; 18: Drawing, Alfred Beaver, Royal Borough of Kensington & Chelsea Library; 19: Painting, Walter Greaves, The Bridgeman Art Library; 20: Photo, James Hedderly, Royal Borough of Kensington & Chelsea Library; 21: NetXPosure Design; 23: Photo, James Hedderly, Royal Borough of Kensington & Chelsea Library; 25: Cabinet UK Limited; 26: Photo, James Hedderly, Royal Borough of Kensington & Chelsea Library; 28: R.Stanford Collection, www.thamestugs.co.uk; 29: S.S.B.R. Archive; 30:

The index for this book was prepared by
Alan Thatcher FSI, ACIB
Sailing barge admirer and professional indexer
56 Foxhill, Olney, Buckinghamshire MK46 5EE
alanthatcher@btopenworld.com

SOCIETY FOR SAILING BARGE RESEARCH   MEMBERSHIP APPLICATION

COMPLETE IN CAPITAL LETTERS AND MAIL TO:

Mrs. M. Blackburn,
Membership Secretary - S.S.B.R.,
Lords Bridge Toll House,
Lordsbridge,
Tilney-cum-Islington,
Kings Lynn,
PE34 3BW

Annual Subscription £15 - enclose cheque payable to Society for Sailing Barge Research or Postal Order/Money Order.

Name(s)..

Address..house name

....number, street

....place name

....post town

....county

....post code   ....country

It may help the Society provide the maximum benefits of membership if you provide the following details. We are committed to complying with the requirements of the Data Protection Act and you will not be sent material other than Society publications and documentation.

Home telephone number..

Work telephone number..

Mobile telephone number...

Email address...

Date of Birth..

Any specific sailing barge interest..

....

....

....